30
YEARS
OF
SOCIAL
CHANGE

Edited by Stephen Jones

Foreword by Jessica Kingsley

Jessica Kingsley *Publishers*
London and Philadelphia

'Shame on the Mental Health System' (Sen 2016) on page 25 reprinted by kind permission of Dolly Sen.

First published in 2018
by Jessica Kingsley Publishers
73 Collier Street
London N1 9BE, UK
and
400 Market Street, Suite 400
Philadelphia, PA 19106, USA

www.jkp.com

Library of Congress Cataloging in Publication Data
A CIP catalog record for this book is available from the Library of Congress

British Library Cataloguing in Publication Data
A CIP catalogue record for this book is available from the British Library

ISBN 978 1 78592 430 9
eISBN 978 1 78450 798 5

Printed and bound in Great Britain

Contents

Foreword

Thirty years is an arbitrary period – a bit more than a generation, a bit less than a working lifetime. This small book marks 30 years of publishing here at JKP, in and around the social and behavioural sciences, with the increasingly explicit goal of helping to create positive social change.

We thought it would be interesting to ask authors from across the areas we have published to write briefly about the changes – for better or worse – they have seen across their area of expertise, and what they might hope (or fear) for the future. And what they say is really interesting. Mostly, things are better; with increasing understanding of conditions such as autism, discrimination and fear has reduced and the autism community (which barely existed 30 years ago) is now a thriving and dynamic source of information, friendship, and support. In social work, the last few years have seen increasing hardship and distress amongst society's poorest, particularly in the UK, but the calibre of work with communities is just amazing in its creativity and understanding of the complex issues, while changes both in the education system and in the challenges facing young people, as well as much better understanding of the requirements of special education, have had a major impact on the teaching profession. Singing Dragon authors have also seen enormous change, in attitudes to and knowledge about acupuncture and Chinese medicine and major developments in the science of aromatherapy, and of nutrition.

As publishers, we have been incredibly fortunate not just to feel that we are contributing to positive change with the books that we have published over those years, but also to work with so many interesting, energetic, and highly creative people, and to have made so many friends with shared values. We are so grateful to all the people who have published with us over the years, and most immediately to those of them who contributed their time to create this interesting book – thank you all!

Jessica Kingsley

22nd September 2017
73 Collier Street, London N1 9BE

1

Fake News, Post-Truth and the Glimmer of Hope

Some Changes in the Educational Landscape, 1987–2017

PAUL COOPER

Imagine, if you can, a world without e-mail, Facebook and Twitter, where the word 'Amazon', for most people, conjures up images of a tropical rainforest and an absolutely enormous river, and 'google' is (if it is anything) the kind of thing that a pre-verbal infant might say to our amusement.

Well, these were just some of the features of life in 1987. This was also a time when most of our reading material came in printed form on paper, and when if you wanted a book to read you would probably have to make a physical journey to a bookshop or library.

If you made the journey by car you would have had to pay something like 38p for a litre of petrol. You would have taken your book home to a house or flat with an average value (in the UK) of £40,000. The idea that Leicester City might one day be one of the most talked about English football clubs throughout the world would have seemed preposterous, as would the possibility that a certain Mr D. Trump might become the most powerful man in the world.

But as Bob Dylan (that surprise recipient for the Nobel Prize for Literature in 2016) once wrote, 'things have changed'.

The Oxford English Dictionary Word of the Year for 2016 was 'post-truth', which is defined as:

> Relating to or denoting circumstances in which objective facts are less influential in shaping public opinion than appeals to emotion and personal belief. (Oxford Living Dictionaries 2017)

This is quite sobering. A major contender for Word (or should that be 'Phrase'?) of the Year 2017 is 'fake news', which is in some ways just another version of 'post-truth', but with the difference that 'fake news' involves the promotion of deliberate falsehoods while 'post-truth' refers to what Michael Gove – who is, at the time of writing, Secretary of State for Environment, Food and Rural Affairs, and let's not forget, a former Secretary of State for *Education* (2010–2014) – demonstrated when, during the EU referendum campaign, he stated that 'people in this country have had enough of experts'.

Together, these words say a lot about the current zeitgeist. It might be argued that one of the greatest differences between 1987 and 2017 is that in the world of the internet, Twitter and fake news people are empowered to make confident decisions on the basis of nothing other than their own or others' 'gut feelings'. If we no longer trust 'experts', then we are freed from the tiresome responsibility of having to justify our opinions through an appeal to evidence. On the other hand, the blind and bland appeal to 'that is what the experts say' is also problematic. After all, experts do not always agree. Thoughtful and informed people do not take claims from anyone at face value; they listen to trusted sources and evaluate the claims of these sources for their validity. Validity often refers to verifiable facts on which the claims are based. In the absence of verifiable factual evidence, the thoughtful person may reserve judgement. The point is that expert opinion is only as good as the evidence on which it is based. The expertise of the expert resides in his/her command of a particular field of evidence-based enquiry.

But there is a growing contempt for evidence. We see this at work in the recent resurgence in the advocacy for grammar schools in England; something that would have seemed unlikely in 1987. Though they have always had their devotees, grammar schools have been shown repeatedly, through research, to reinforce rather than ameliorate the negative effects of socio-economic disadvantage (Andrews, Hutchinson and Johnes 2016; LSE 2014; Sutton Trust 2014). It would probably have surprised people in 1987 to learn that studies of social mobility, which inevitably take considerable time to complete because of their reliance on longitudinal data, by 'expert' organizations including the Sutton Trust in the UK, demonstrate a marked decline in social mobility since 1977 (Sutton Trust 2007).

The reasons for this are multifarious, but they tend to coalesce around what has come to be referred to as the rise of neoliberalism. This is an ideological (as opposed to evidence-based) political philosophy which applies the principles of consumer–provider economics to almost everything, including public services such as education and health. The poverty of this ideology when applied to education (and health, for that matter) lies in its bland and ignorant assumptions that the quality of outcomes is easy to define, and all consumers are equally well equipped to make the kinds of choices that make markets work.

For example, where I live I have the choice of shopping at a variety of local supermarkets, including the established 'big name' ones and the so-called 'budget' ones. I use them all. I have learned, over many years, that 'brand loyalty' is a bogus concept. I shop for quality and value and do my best to avoid being seduced by the cheap gimmicks that all supermarkets employ. In 1987 it would probably have been deemed absurd to point out that schools are very different from supermarkets. Not so in 2017. Over the past 30 years there have been a variety of UK governmental interventions, including the 1988 Education Reform Act (ERA), the establishment of Ofsted, the introduction of performance league tables and the introduction of academies and free schools. A major feature of the ERA was the introduction of the National Curriculum (NC). The NC is, by definition, a standardised curriculum, though it is only compulsory for local authority-run schools. It took a while for it to sink in for some of us that a major purpose behind the NC was (and is) to create a platform for making market-type comparisons between schools. To put it plainly, this approach to education enables consumer comparisons. The analogy is: supermarket A sells the same brand of bread at £1, while supermarket B sells the same product at 75p. So, supermarket B offers better value, in relation to bread at least. It follows that if school A achieves higher levels of performance in public examinations than school B, then school A is where you should send your child. This approach came to be applied to SATs results, GCSE results and A level results.

Then there were the international comparison tables, the most well known of which is the OECD's Programme for International Student Assessment (PISA) which many governments throughout the world imbue with uncritical trust. Oddly, Michael Gove was, as Secretary of State for Education, utterly trusting of PISA, in spite of his apparent distaste for expert opinion. In fact, on the basis of PISA results, he urged British teachers to adopt the teaching methods applied in Hong Kong and South Korea. These teaching methods tend to emphasise whole-group teaching, rote learning and minimal student participation.

So what's wrong with whole-group teaching, rote learning and minimal student participation? The short answer to this question is that this kind of pedagogy encourages the uncritical consumption of information, and in doing so feeds the uncritical consumption of 'fake news' and 'post-truth' culture. It is the pedagogy of docility and disempowerment, encouraging classrooms in which students' natural curiosity is curtailed in favour of predefined and 'approved' content. Teachers in this kind of pedagogic regime become the implementers of predefined curricula, as opposed to being creative and sensitive mentors to growing minds (see Black and Deci 2000; Cooper and McIntyre 1996; Deci and Ryan 1987; Ryan and Deci 2000).

But is it all bad? Have the past 30 years been such a disaster in education? Well, no. And the key words here are 'mental health'. This phrase was well established in some circles in 1987, but less so in education. It is a wonderful thing that the mental health agenda has grown in prominence to the point where it is now a major feature of contemporary social and educational policy debates. It is possible that, through this development, schools will become places where respect for humanity finally becomes central to the theory and practice of education. This could be the greatest challenge to the crude, Darwinian mentality which has come to dominate our education system. Human beings thrive when they are nurtured. This is true of families and it is equally true of schools.

It is my hope that the late (but welcome) dawning of this realisation will contribute to the much-needed transformation of schools. This is not a short-term hope but a long-term vision. We can do better in the education of our children, and we must. If we replace the impulse to coerce and mould our children with the commitment to caring for and listening to them, then we will begin to unleash their natural enthusiasm for learning and cultivate their social-emotional awareness and problem-solving abilities.

If these things happen we can look forward to a better world. I look forward to that world.

References

Andrews, J., Hutchinson, J. and Johnes, R. (2016) *Grammar Schools and Social Mobility*. London: Education Policy Unit. https://epi.org.uk/wp-content/uploads/2016/09/Grammar-schools-and-social-mobility_.pdf (accessed 12 July 2017).

Black, A. and Deci, E. (2000) 'Organic chemistry: A self-determination theory perspective.' *Science Education 84*, 6, 740–756.

Cooper, P. and McIntyre, D. (1996) *Effective Teaching and Learning: Teacher and Student Perceptions*. Buckingham: Open University Press.

Deci, E. and Ryan, R. (1987) 'The support of autonomy and the control of behavior.' *Journal of Personality and Social Psychology 53*, 1024–1037.

LSE (2014) 'Why Grammar Schools Are No Quick Fix for England's Social Mobility Problems.' http://blogs.lse.ac.uk/politicsandpolicy/why-grammar-schools-are-no-quick-fix-for-englands-social-mobility-problems (accessed 12 July 2017).

Oxford Living Dictionaries (2017) 'Word of the Year 2016 Is...' Oxford: Oxford University Press. https://en.oxforddictionaries.com/word-of-the-year/word-of-the-year-2016 (accessed 6 July 2017).

Ryan, R. and Deci, E. (2000) 'Self-determination theory and the facilitation of intrinsic motivation, social development, and well-being.' *American Psychologist 55*, 68–78.

Sutton Trust (2007) 'Low Social Mobility in the UK Has Not Improved in 30 Years.' www.suttontrust.com/newsarchive/low-social-mobility-uk-improved-30-years (accessed 12 July 2017).

Sutton Trust (2014) 'Grammar School is No Better for Pupils than a Comprehensive.' www.suttontrust.com/newsarchive/grammar-school-is-no-better-for-pupils-than-a-comprehensive (accessed 12 July 2017).

* * *

PAUL COOPER, PhD, CPsychol, FBPsS, is Emeritus Professor, Brunel University London, and Visiting Professor at the Centre for Resilience and Socio-Emotional Health, University of Malta. Over the past 30-plus years he has held academic posts at Birmingham, Oxford, Cambridge and Leicester universities and the Hong Kong Institute of Education (where he was Associate Vice President, Quality Assurance). His research and publications are concerned with social-emotional learning, mental health and learning and teaching in schools. He has published many books and articles on these topics. He is a past editor (now honorary associate editor) of the journal *Emotional and Behavioural Difficulties*, and is co-editor of *The International Journal of Emotional Education*. He is also an Honorary Life Vice President of the Social, Emotional and Behavioural Difficulties Association (SEBDA). Prior to working in universities he was a school teacher. *Attachment and Emotional Development in the Classroom: Theory and Practice*, edited by David Colley and Paul Cooper, is also published by Jessica Kingsley Publishers.

2

Gender Diversity

CJ ATKINSON

To ask how the world has changed in 30 years is a little bit like asking a baker how different a bag of flour or six eggs is once it has turned into a cake. In the past 30 years, the ways that we talk about gender have grown and evolved from challenging gender inequalities to questioning the very notion of gender identity and gender expression. Heroes of queer activism and theory, such as Susan Stryker, Leslie Feinberg, Kate Bornstein and S. Bear Bergman, have written seminal texts about gender, gender identity and the changing landscape of the self, which have helped to shape and form a rapidly developing discourse.

Even in the few years that I've been involved with activism, the conversation has progressed at breakneck speed, as people test the limits of language and exalt in the feelings of hard-fought freedoms: freedoms which are more than a rhetorical device. Legislative and policy changes have decriminalised our bodies and begun to provide basic legal protections. The 2003 repeal of Section 28 – a law in the UK which prohibited any discussions of LGBTQ existence in schools – has led to a steady increase in inclusive education.

Even with the progress made, this education is still in its infancy – the systems put in place to help and to serve, from schools to the NHS to the prison system, are failing transgender people. Similarly, activists in the US fight for rights and recognition which fluctuate on a federal and state level, often changing from week to week. There is always a fight and the concessions are often grudging, as questions of gender are still being asked and debated by those who know very little about the topic.

For all of the struggle, it has been the power and resilience of transgender people that have continued to make the difference to transgender representation over the past 30 years. The advent of the internet and the strength of social media turned 2014 into a bell that rang out loudly and clearly, as transgender issues entered the public consciousness. Thanks to the high profiles of transgender women such as Laverne Cox, Janet Mock and Caitlyn Jenner, the existence of transgender people entered people's everyday lives on a scale that simply hadn't been seen before.

This visibility has bred a specific kind of vulnerability. Attacks are made on the existence or appropriateness of transgender people regularly: in the press, on the internet, across social media and in everyday conversation, as though existence can be debated away. A preoccupation with sexual orientation and genitalia often walks hand in hand with the erroneous belief that gender-variant people have never existed before. Yet the history of trans and gender-variant people stretches back much further than we have ever been led to believe and, consistently, trans and gender-variant people have been erased from a communal history.

In many ways this has created a shorthand that 'transgender people' explicitly means 'transgender women'. It targets members of the community who seem to be the easiest to 'other', or the easiest to detect. The casual erasure of the transmasculine experience is something which is new and troubling, but is a reminder that a movement is never complete. It is 2017 and the statistics on mental wellbeing and happiness for young trans people continue to make stark reading. Young trans people are still more likely to suffer from bullying, discrimination, sexual assault and homelessness. One in two trans young people will consider suicide, and one in three will attempt it. While the world has continued to evolve and change over the past 30 years, there's no secret that we still have plenty of work to do.

Whatever happens from here on out, the excuses for ignorance and injustice no longer wash. A generation of children – the generation after me – will grow up in a world where a body doesn't have to feel like a prison sentence. They will grow up in a world where, thanks to the pioneers of a movement who have been fighting to survive, they can be free to exist as themselves. As younger people claim their agency and tell the stories of their own lives and existences, the opportunities for growth exist everywhere.

There's a temptation always to say 'Look how far we've come', as though rights are immutable and immoveable. The current political climate in the US is a reminder that, for every celebration of freedom, we are only ever moments away from these rights being removed. The inalienable rights of the everyday citizen are not currently extended to all of us.

Make no mistake, the reason I and others like me consider ourselves activists is because this is a question of life and death. The world still seems incapable of allowing humans to live intersectional lives, as people of colour – and particularly trans women of colour – bear the heavier burden of discrimination, alienation, incarceration, risk of physical violence, and murder. As young people identify more and more with looser notions of gender and identity, the potential for the future is exhilarating and exciting. It blows the future wide open for who it is that might take the reins and how it might evolve. If there's any enduring legacy of the work that's being done, it's that there's no way to predict where the conversation will go in another 30 years, only that it will go on.

* * *

CJ ATKINSON is a queer writer, educator and trans activist. CJ's first book, *Can I Tell You About Gender Diversity?* (Jessica Kingsley Publishers, 2017), is designed to help young people talk about gender variance. CJ writes regularly about the marginalisation and erasure of the transmasculine and genderqueer experience, and is currently working on a PhD in poetry and queer theory.

3

Mental Health Stigma

Talking and Taboo?

SARAH CARR

Thirty years ago, I was in the midst of my first introduction to the workings of stigma, which consequently introduced me to the importance of activism. I was in my mid-teens, and Margaret Thatcher had just won her third general election. In December 1987 the Section 28 amendment of the Local Government Act was introduced into Parliament by Jill Knight, Tory MP for Birmingham Edgbaston, and David Wilshire, Tory MP for Spelthorne. The amendment was as follows:

> 2A – (1) A local authority shall not –
>
> a) intentionally promote homosexuality or publish material with the intention of promoting homosexuality;

b) promote the teaching in any maintained scl
of the acceptability of homosexuality a
pretended family relationship.

Thorp and Allen 2000, p.7

Finally repealed by the New Labour Government in
2003 (Gillan 2003), Section (or Clause) 28 represented
the political stigmatisation of a social group. It literally
legislated for their silencing. I was a member of that group
and, like many others at the time, my response was to resist
stigmatisation. In 1988 I went alone to join my very first
protest march: the 'Stop the Clause' march on Parliament.
We declared, along with our comrades in Leeds (Ward
2014), Manchester (Lansley 2013) and other parts of the
UK, that we were 'Never Going Underground'.

Contrary to the Government's wishes, Section 28 had
the effect of galvanising activism among lesbian, gay and
bisexual people. Famously, several gay women abseiled into
the House of Lords (Direct Action 2016a) during the vote
and disrupted a BBC live news broadcast (Direct Action
2016b) on the evening the law was passed. In 1988 the
anti-Section 28 Gay Pride march saw record attendance
as lesbian, gay and bisexual people and allies mobilised
en masse in protest. Across the country, community-run
help lines and mutual support groups sprang up for people
managing the process of coming out. All this sent out the
defiant message: you may try to stigmatise us, but you won't
shame or silence us.

Thirty years on, I find myself in a similar position as a
member of a different group that is being morally and socially
stigmatised, and by another Tory government: people living
with and managing mental distress. Many are being given
a mark of disgrace as sick 'skivers and scroungers', just as

lesbian, gay and bisexual people were politically marked as sick 'deviants and perverts'. However, the definitions and experiences of stigma for mental health are perhaps more complex and ambiguous than they were for lesbian, gay and bisexual people in 1987.

In 1987, many people with long-term mental health problems were literally being 'kept in the closet', that is, forcibly segregated from society in hospitals and long-stay psychiatric institutions. It is worth noting that some of these people will also have been lesbian, gay or bisexual as homosexuality was still classified as a mental disorder in the International Classification of Diseases (ICD), and did not completely disappear from the psychiatric Diagnostic and Statistical Manual (DSM) until 1987. The large-scale institutional closures did not start until the late 1980s, when people who had lived in institutions were moved out into community settings (Gilburt and Peck 2014). However, public fear about 'dangerousness', targeted victimisation and NIMBY (not in my backyard) campaigns heralded a new era of stigma and discrimination for people with mental health problems who were living in the community (Gray 2002).

Stigma and discrimination are a consistent and key issue in mental health. Over the past few years, awareness and definitions of mental health stigma have been largely determined by government-funded charities, media campaigns, global psychiatry, academics from clinical and social scientific disciplines and, most recently, the new generation of English Royals and the current prime minister, Theresa May. 'Respectable' people with mental health problems are being encouraged to come out and talk about their experiences, and celebrities are telling their personal stories. We are told that mental distress is an illness, like any other, and that one in four of us will experience mental health problems at some point in our lives. Much of this anti-stigma activity is laudable, and has been effective in changing certain public attitudes to individuals with mental health problems. However, the stigma campaign concept is heavily curated by PR and campaign departments of large national charities. They tend to favour individual stories of overcoming 'mental illness' and of recovering socio-economic 'functionality' – that is, going into paid work or having a relationship and family.

Despite these campaigns, those living with mental distress remain subject to stigmatising processes in the welfare benefits system, mental health services and the workplace, with a UK study into mental health-related stigma and discrimination concluding that 'the welfare benefits system has become an increasing source of discriminatory experience' (Henderson *et al.* 2014, p.1599). As funding for disability benefits and care packages is reduced, so people's risk of crisis increases, leaving them exposed and open to potential victimisation by neighbours, or at risk of being publicly detained by the police under Section 136 of the Mental Health Act. In government discussions on welfare policy, people with mental health problems have been characterised as the fake disabled (Stewart 2017).

For those in work, the Government and employers are promoting 'mindfulness' policies to encourage individual workers to think positively (Mindfulness APPG 2015), while ignoring the risks posed by poor physical and psychosocial working conditions that are inaccessible or damaging to people with mental health problems, with chronic stress, bullying and discrimination. Some clinicians are recognising the uncomfortable silence around the stigma perpetuated in mental health services and by mental health staff (Thornicroft *et al.* 2015), an issue that is being brought to the surface and addressed in research and mainstream anti-stigma campaigns (Henderson *et al.* 2014).

I would argue that this structural and institutional stigmatisation is being strategically used by a neoliberal Tory government and, despite the fact that it is causing widespread damage, it hardly ever features in mainstream anti-stigma campaigns.

So, in high-profile public campaigns, there are some things we are positively being encouraged to talk about in the context of combating mental health stigma, and some things we're not. We are permitted to talk about overcoming depression and returning to work, but we're not supported to talk openly about things like being driven to suicidal crisis by benefits sanctions; workplace bullying; abuse in psychiatric services; or living with the trauma of violence and abuse or in chronic poverty with poor housing.

In the context of this obvious dissonance, is the concept of stigma still politically useful for mental health service users, survivors and their organisations?

If we accept the dictionary definition of stigma as a 'mark of disgrace' (English Oxford Living Dictionaries 2017), we have to ask, who is marking us, how and why? Arguably stigma comes from what other people feel about you, but how does 'being marked' make *you* feel? The survivor artist and activist Dolly Sen offers an answer to this question through her 'Prescription of Shame' (Sen 2015). Shame can be defined as the painful feeling of humiliation and distress – it is how you are made to feel about yourself. As this poem shows, Dolly is very explicit about the shaming nature of psychiatric treatment:

SHAME ON THE MENTAL HEALTH SYSTEM

Tell us your shame
Tell me your most shameful secrets
You are not going to tell me?
Then you must be sick.

You need treatment.
You need my expertise.
My expertise means I can have no shame
I can hide it
But you must always tell me yours when you see me.
Must I restrain you to protect me from myself?
Here, have more shame to drown you.

You must engage.
You must engage in your shaming.
I don't know why you are not getting any better.

Sen 2016

Popular and PR-driven anti-stigma campaigns are becoming detached from the reality of the shaming of those who experience mental distress, most of whom already struggle with personal shame. They avoid engaging with structural, institutional and economic stigmatisation and the shaming effects it has on tens of thousands of people, their families, friends and communities. So, while mainstream charities, academics, celebrities and politicians are talking about stigma, mental health service users and survivors are beginning to talk about *shame*. David Gilbert, former mental health service user and patient and public engagement practitioner, has said in his blog, 'A campaign to tell us to talk more openly may risk exacerbating our feelings of shame – and shame is a huge issue for us' (Gilbert 2017).

Just as lesbian, gay and bisexual people were galvanised into action when they were the focus of strategic political stigmatisation by a Tory government, many mental health service users and survivors are responding with radical activism (see e.g. RecoveryintheBin:https://recoveryinthebin.org) and direct action (see e.g. the Mental Health Resistance Network: http://mentalhealthresistance.org), and adopting clear political positions on the wider effects of austerity and neoliberal policies, as well as psychiatry (NSUN 2017). As part of resisting structural and institutional stigmatisation, some activists are resisting the big anti-stigma campaigns (Gilbert 2017) that no longer represent our real experiences or interests. Thirty years on from 1987 the defiant message can be heard once again: 'You may try to stigmatise us, but you won't shame or silence us.'

The views in this chapter are solely those of the author, and not those of the institution or organisation she is affiliated with.

References

Direct Action (2016a, 10 May) Lesbians Abseiling into House of Lords Protest Section 28 Clause 28 [Video file]. www.youtube.com/watch?v=LoTtl8hNBNk (accessed 28 July 2017).

Direct Action (2016b, 11 May) Central Weekend Live with Women who Invaded 6 O'Clock News in Protest of Section 28 [Video file]. www.youtube.com/watch?v=Sk3hU7xx2oI (accessed 28 July 2017).

English Oxford Living Dictionaries (2017) 'Stigma.' Oxford: Oxford University Press. https://en.oxforddictionaries.com/definition/stigma (accessed 28 July 2017).

Gilbert, D. (2017, 29 April) 'Let's (not) talk about depression.' Future Patient – Musing on Patient-Led Healthcare [Blog post]. https://futurepatientblog.com/2017/04/29/lets-not-talk-about-depression (accessed 28 July 2017).

Gilburt, H. and Peck, E. (2014) *Service Transformation: Lessons in Mental Health.* London: The King's Fund.

Gillan, A. (2003) 'Section 28 gone…but not forgotten.' *The Guardian*, 17 November. www.theguardian.com/politics/2003/nov/17/uk.gayrights (accessed 28 July 2017).

Gray, A. (2002) 'Stigma in psychiatry.' *Journal of the Royal Society of Medicine 95*, 2, 72–76.

Henderson, R. C., Corker, E., Hamilton, S., Williams, P. *et al.* (2014) 'Viewpoint survey of mental health service users' experiences of discrimination in England 2008–2012.' *Social Psychiatry and Psychiatric Epidemiology 49*, 10, 1599–1608.

Lansley, N. (2013, 30 March) Manchester Stop Clause 28 / Never Going Underground / Gay Rights Rally [Video file]. www.youtube.com/watch?v=pbNig5ZNgTE (accessed 28 July 2017).

Mindfulness APPG (2015) *Mindful Nation UK.* Report by the Mindfulness All Party Parliamentary Group. London: Mindfulness Initiative. http://themindfulnessinitiative.org.uk/images/reports/Mindfulness-APPG-Report_Mindful-Nation-UK_Oct2015.pdf (accessed 28 July 2017).

National Survivor User Network (NSUN) (2017) *NSUN Manifesto 2017.* London: NSUN.

Sen, D. (2015, 15 September) 'Shame on the mental health system/15 September 2015.' Disability Arts Online [Blog post]. www.disabilityartsonline.org.uk/dolly_sen_blog?item=2606 (accessed 28 July 2017).

Sen, D. (2016) 'Shame on the Mental Health System.' In *DSM 69: Dolly Sen's Manual of Psychiatric Disorder.* London: Eleusinian Press.

Stewart, H. (2017) 'May adviser regrets saying benefits should only go to "really disabled" people.' *The Guardian*, 27 February. www.theguardian.com/politics/2017/feb/27/may-adviser-george-freeman-regrets-benefits-disabled-people-anxiety (accessed 28 July 2017).

Thornicroft, G., Mehta, N., Clement, S., Evans-Lacko, S. *et al.* (2015) 'Evidence for effective interventions to reduce mental-health-related stigma and discrimination.' *The Lancet Psychiatry 387*, 10023, 1123–1132.

Thorp, A. and Allen, G. (2000) *The Local Government Bill [HL]: The 'Section 28' Debate.* Research Paper 00.47. London: House of Commons Library.

Ward, J. (2014, 6 November) Stop the Clause Demos 1987/1988 [Video file]. https://vimeo.com/78726513 (accessed 28 July 2017).

* * *

SARAH CARR is Associate Professor of Mental Health Research and Co-Director of the Centre for Co-production in Mental Health at Middlesex University London. She also runs her own independent mental health and social care knowledge consultancy. She has experience of mental distress and mental health service use and uses this to inform all her work. Sarah is Vice Chair of the National Survivor User Network

(NSUN) and a member of the editorial boards of *Disability and Society* and *The Lancet Psychiatry*. In 2012 she co-edited (with Professor Peter Beresford) the book *Social Care, Service Users and User Involvement*, published by Jessica Kingsley Publishers, and was a member of the NICE Guideline Development Group for NICE CG136: *Service User Experience in Adult Mental Health*. Sarah is a Fellow of the Royal Society of Arts, Honorary Senior Lecturer at the School for Social Policy, Birmingham University, and Visiting Fellow at the School of Social Policy and Social Work at the University of York.

4

The Stigma of Autism

LUKE BEARDON

As Jessica Kingsley Publishers celebrate their thirtieth anniversary, I consider how stigma relating to autism has changed over that time; has it, in fact, changed? Are we any better off in 2017 compared to 1987 – or even before then? One might assume that over the decades the world has changed considerably when it comes to an understanding of autism. But is this really the case?

'Refrigerator parenting'

Even back in the 1940s one of the pioneers of autism, psychiatrist Leo Kanner, was (presumably inadvertently) stigmatising autism. In his case, famously perpetuated by psychoanalyst Bruno Bettelheim, this stigma was directed at the parents, specifically mothers, of autistic children, who were blamed as the cause of the autism resulting from a lack of maternal warmth. They were labelled 'refrigerator mothers'. Through people like Leo Kanner and Bruno Bettelheim, the notion that autism was somehow caused by poor parenting was born. One might scoff at such nonsense in this day and age, but be careful in assuming that such dangerous notions no longer exist. To this day an oft required or suggested 'support' for parents of autistic families is to invite them for 'family therapy' – does this really help, or does it continue to hint at the problems stemming from parenting? How many parents are routinely made to feel that problems at school must be based on problems at home? How many parents are made to feel that any problems associated with their child are synonymous with poor parenting? Autism – still stigmatised? Yes.

The triad of impairments

I'd argue that Lorna Wing and Judith Gould's ground-breaking paper in 1979 on the triad of impairments in people with autism – impairments of social interaction, social language and communication, and social imagination – is a truly seminal paper. I have the utmost respect for both authors, but this deficit-based model of autism has been challenged over and over again by academics (including myself) and, far more importantly, by publications from members of the autism community, as evidenced in ethnographic writings and memoirs (some of the first ever were published by JKP) as well as through blogs, vlogs and online support groups. Many refute the deficit-based model, using the social model to articulate autism as a neurological variance, or difference, rather than deficit. I have argued for years that while being autistic might put a person at a distinct disadvantage it is not, inherently, a disorder or impairment. In a presentation last week I had a slide suggesting 'The PNT (predominant neurotype) are extremely impaired autistics, just as autistics might be fairly poor at being non-autistics, despite trying really hard.' I don't think that comparing one group with the other is at all justified, nor fair.

So, recently, there has been some movement towards an acceptance that being autistic isn't necessarily the tragedy that a medical deficit- and impairment-based model might suggest. And yet the current diagnostic criteria in the DSM-5 (American Psychiatric Association 2013) still subscribe to a medical model of autism, ensuring that to 'qualify' for a diagnosis, autism must be problematised in the first instance. Terms such as 'deficit' and 'impairment' litter the criteria. Autism – still stigmatised? Yes.

Public awareness of autism

From *Rainman* through to *The A-Word*, the media has picked up that autism sells – so is this the breakthrough that the autism community has been waiting for? Are shows such as *The Undateables* truly representative, or are autistic individuals still presented as savant-like geniuses, characters to pity or – even worse – a source of amusement for the general populace? The *Beyond Rainman* report by the National Autistic Society (1996), which ascertained levels of awareness in the general population in 1996, is starkly contrasted by their 2015 report (YouGov 2015), which suggested that 99 per cent of the population were 'aware' of autism. But so what? What does 'being aware' mean, and how much value is there in just being 'aware'? Why aren't terms such as 'autism *understanding*' or 'autism *acceptance*' at the forefront of our minds instead? Huge amounts of research grants go into seeking a cause, even a cure. What message does that send to the autism community, and to society?

JKP was one of the first publishers to proactively support autistic adults to get autobiographical accounts published. The promotion of the autistic voice is one of the most important and valuable movements ever to have existed in the autism field. The many examples of autobiographical writing on autism, autistic speakers at conferences, autistic academics, and bloggers and vloggers on autism is a welcome and long overdue addition to the body of knowledge about autism, though autistic voices still remain under-represented in the wider public arena. The way in which society learns about autism is slowly changing – though still far too slowly. Autism – still stigmatised? Yes.

Over the years there have been all sorts of 'therapies' designed to either 'cure' autism or make a person 'less autistic'. From diets to detox to secretin injections, parents have been subjected to unethical practice with no evidence base, sometimes to devastating effect. Of course one would think that society no longer blankly accepts quack therapies, latest trends and costly interventions as valid – or does it? Just this week reports of bleach ingestion as an autism cure were all over social media. Autism – still stigmatised? Yes.

Autism in the future

So, what does the future hold? Will autism always be associated with negativity? Will there always be an air of the tragic surrounding the diagnosis or identification of a child? Will a medical model always prevail over a social model in relation to autism? Will baseless assumptions always be made about autistic individuals simply because they happen to be autistic?

I genuinely believe that a categorical 'No' should be the answer to all of these questions. In order to counterbalance the stigma of autism, all those involved in the autism world should support the work of advocates for the autism community, including JKP, in promoting the autistic voice. For me, this means continuing to collate stories for publication in JKP's 'Insider Intelligence' series, which has five publications under its proverbial belt with several autistic voices represented. So far, the series has addressed the autistic experiences of: social relationships, employment, mental health, positive experiences, and intimate relationships.

In my day job teaching an autism course, it means supporting autistic students to the best of my ability and teaching whoever will listen about all things related to autism, while continuing to learn myself. It means continuing to provide a platform for autistic speakers to contribute to the course and have their voices heard. It means continuing to write and publish with autistic co-authors in academic journals.

One of my favourite autistic writers is an Australian woman called Alyssa Aleksanian. In *Bittersweet on the Autism Spectrum*, published by JKP, she writes, 'The privilege of being oneself is a gift many take for granted, but for someone with AS [Asperger's syndrome], being *allowed* to be oneself is the greatest and rarest gift of all' (Beardon and Worton 2017, p.20).

This is both a poignant and stunning piece of writing, but heartbreaking at the same time. Imagine a world where such is the stigma of being one's self that the *greatest and rarest gift* is to be 'allowed' simply to be you. This is the world that many autistic people still find themselves in to this very day. And that world needs to change – I do think it is in the process of changing.

The stigma of autism; one day it will be a nasty historical relic, rightly banished to distant memory. Until then, there is much work to do.

References

American Psychiatric Association (2013) *Diagnostic and Statistical Manual of Mental Disorders, 5th Edition: DSM-5*. Washington, DC: American Psychiatric Association.

Beardon, L. and Worton, D. (2017) *Bittersweet on the Autism Spectrum*. London: Jessica Kingsley Publishers.

National Autistic Society (1996) *Beyond Rainman*. London: National Autistic Society.

Wing, L. and Gould, J. (1979) 'Severe impairments of social interaction and associated abnormalities in children: Epidemiology and classification.' *Journal of Autism and Developmental Disorders 9*, 11–29.

YouGov (2015) 'More people in the UK are aware of autism.' https://yougov.co.uk/news/2015/04/13/more-people-uk-are-aware-autism (accessed 25 July 2017).

★ ★ ★

LUKE BEARDON has been working for decades in the autism field, in capacities ranging from practitioner to researcher to trainer. His current post is with Sheffield Hallam University, as senior lecturer in autism, and course leader for the Postgraduate Certificate in Autism and Asperger Syndrome, run in collaboration with the National Autistic Society. Luke has written extensively on autism and Asperger's syndrome, and has co-edited five books on autism and Asperger's syndrome published by Jessica Kingsley Publishers. His latest book is *Autism and Asperger Syndrome in Adults* (Sheldon Press, 2017).

5

How Our Understanding of and Approach to Autism Has Developed Over 30 Years

TONY ATTWOOD

Autism is caused by an emotionally cold mother and is an expression of schizophrenia. That was the opinion of psychiatrists and psychologists from the 1950s to the early 1970s. Autism was perceived as a rare and profound disability, with autistic children frequently admitted to institutions for the remainder of their lives. This was the world of autism when I was a psychology student in the early 1970s. In my role as a volunteer at a special school in England, I met two aloof and non-verbal children with a diagnosis of autism. I found their characteristics both entrancing and intriguing, and from that point, as a first-year student, I resolved to become a specialist in autism.

During the 1980s there was a paradigm shift in terms of the conceptualisation of autism as a neurodevelopmental disorder affecting the connections and functioning of specific areas of the brain, rather than a disorder caused by faulty parenting and an expression of psychosis. There was also the recognition of a much wider range of expression of autism, including Asperger's syndrome. New and effective diagnostic assessment instruments and therapies to improve specific abilities were developed.

When Jessica Kingsley Publishers was founded 30 years ago, there was a growing need for literature for parents, professionals and those who have autism. JKP became the right publisher at the right time, producing the seminal books on so many aspects of autism, particularly Asperger's syndrome. In the latter part of the 1980s, the landscape of autism was changing rapidly: there were new insights from autobiographies; research into the social challenges faced by those who have autism; exploration of the language profile; and the development of education and therapy programmes for use at both school and home. The residential institutions were being closed, families were provided with support, and there was encouragement for children with autism to be integrated into their local schools.

During the 1990s there was an increasing need for literature on the circumstances, abilities and support needs for adults with autism, and particularly Asperger's syndrome. There was also a proliferation of diagnostic instruments, research using neuroimaging and studies on the causes and genetics of autism. There was a recognition that autism could be associated with mood disorders, especially anxiety, and an acknowledged profile of social abilities and difficulties.

In the millennium years, JKP published increasingly diverse literature, addressing such issues as strategies to improve friendship and relationship skills, the sensory profile associated with autism, programmes for sexuality education, and the unique abilities and experiences of girls and women who have Asperger's syndrome. These years also saw the proliferation of children receiving a diagnosis of an autism spectrum disorder (ASD), with the previous estimate of autism as occurring in one child in 2500 changing to one child in 68 (Centers for Disease Control and Prevention 2017). While the increase could be attributed to a greater accuracy in diagnosing autism and the inclusion of a wider range of expression of ASD, my thoughts are that there has been a genuine but modest increase in the prevalence of autism, though we have yet to explain why. The millennium years were also associated with the growth of a significant self-advocacy movement, and with literature on both employment and college education. There was a move to explain the characteristics of ASD to children, which included a range of stories and novels with the central character having Asperger's syndrome.

In 1998, my book *Asperger's Syndrome: A Guide for Parents and Professionals* reviewed about 180 research studies and books on Asperger's syndrome. By 2006, however, my *Complete Guide to Asperger's Syndrome* reviewed over 500 research studies and publications – clear evidence of a huge increase in research and knowledge.

Since 2013, there has been a reduction in the rate of diagnosis of ASD due to both changed and stricter diagnostic criteria. The term 'Asperger's syndrome' has been formally replaced with the term 'Autism Spectrum Disorder – Level 1 without accompanying intellectual or language impairment' (American Psychiatric Association 2013, p.51). I continue to use the term Asperger's syndrome for simplicity and continuity.

There has also been a greater recognition of the need to identify girls who have Asperger's syndrome, with a probable male:female ratio of 2:1. The girls are more creative and effective than the boys in camouflaging their social confusion by careful observation, analysis and imitation of social abilities. JKP have now published a range of books specifically for girls and women with Asperger's syndrome. There has also been the development and evaluation of therapy programmes for mood disorders, such as my self-help book *Exploring Depression, and Beating the Blues* (2016), written with my colleague Michelle Garnett. Research studies have explored the very early signs of autism in infants, characteristics associated with autism in parents and siblings, strategies to support inclusive education as well as home schooling, and issues associated with seeking and maintaining employment.

There has also been research and literature on specific aspects of sexuality, such as the higher than expected level of gender dysphoria associated with ASD, and examination of the level of substance abuse, often due to self-medication in order to manage anxiety. Once again, JKP have been at the forefront in publishing literature that reflects and encourages our developing understanding of autism and strategies to develop specific abilities.

Having explored the landscape of autism for over 40 years, what do I believe are the likely areas of discovery in the future?

We will need to know more about ageing and autism. Do the characteristics change over time? How should we educate those involved in services for the aged about the needs of someone with autism?

Another fascinating area is that of actually un-diagnosing ASD. My own clinical practice and longitudinal research indicates that perhaps around 15 per cent of those who receive a diagnosis of ASD in early childhood can and do achieve many of those abilities that parents and teachers thought would always be elusive. The characteristics of autism can eventually become sub-clinical for a growing proportion of adults who have ASD. It is interesting that the positive characteristics, such as a talent in mathematics or drawing, do not diminish, but the social puzzle of life is finally solved and the person learns to live with, and adapt to, the more troublesome characteristics such as sensory sensitivity and anxiety.

This newly recognised prognosis no doubt has many explanations, but one of these is surely greater knowledge, which has been the intention and value of Jessica Kingsley Publishers.

References

American Psychiatric Association (2013) *Diagnostic and Statistical Manual of Mental Disorders, 5th Edition: DSM-5*. Washington, DC: American Psychiatric Association.

Attwood, T. (1998) *Asperger's Syndrome: A Guide for Parents and Professionals*. London: Jessica Kingsley Publishers.

Attwood, T. (2006) *The Complete Guide to Asperger's Syndrome*. London: Jessica Kingsley Publishers.

Attwood, T. and Garnett, M. (2016) *Exploring Depression, and Beating the Blues*. London: Jessica Kingsley Publishers.

Centers for Disease Control and Prevention (2017) 'Autism Spectrum Disorder (ASD): Data and Statistics.' www.cdc.gov/ncbddd/autism/data.html (accessed 19 July 2017).

* * *

TONY ATTWOOD is a clinical psychologist from Brisbane, Australia, with over 40 years of experience as a clinician with individuals with ASDs. He is Adjunct Professor at Griffith University in Queensland, senior consultant at the Minds and Hearts clinic in Brisbane, and author of *The Complete Guide to Asperger's Syndrome* (Jessica Kingsley Publishers, 2006). He has developed and evaluated a range of therapy programmes specifically designed for children, adolescents and adults with autism spectrum disorder, and the author of research papers on many aspects of ASD, including the diagnosis of girls and adults with ASD.

6

What I Have Learnt Over Three Decades as a Child and Adolescent Psychiatrist

NISHA DOGRA

I have been working as a child and adolescent psychiatrist for over 25 years. It is a clinical discipline that I have never regretted entering, but it is a discipline that is under more pressure than I have ever known. Despite the various campaigns that have taken place, stigma associated with mental health remains commonplace and, despite all the rhetoric and claims, mental health services remain underfunded. For *child* mental health services the situation is worse. We are nowhere near a point where there is parity between funding for child physical health and child mental health.

While practising community paediatrics I found the most appealing part of the job to be the psychological component. I vividly recall seeing an eight-year-old boy in a school clinic with recurrent abdominal pain; within 15 minutes we had established that he was being bullied at school and that this was the cause of his pain. In some ways, this could be termed a minor success; it was not a huge surprise to discover that a child's recurrent abdominal pain might have psychological origins. However, it could also be considered a *major* success considering he had seen several other clinicians who had failed to identify the cause of the pain.

This experience really drove home to me how so much of psychiatry is dependent on the clinical skills of the doctor. I enjoyed the challenge of developing my interviewing skills, especially with children. Psychiatry, if done properly, requires the psychiatrist to be aware of so many different factors and constantly reflect on and be aware of the difference between their own experience and influences and those of the patient.

Some years ago I saw a young lady who might be described as a 'difficult' patient. She was 17 with a horrendous family history of abuse and neglect. She was difficult to engage but we managed to do so, and she left our service doing okay. About three years after her discharge I received a letter from her. She was moving, and in packing up her things she had come across the letters that I had written about her and to her as her psychiatrist. She felt it was important to let us know that she recognised the value of the service we had provided because she was in a better place in her life – somewhere she had never expected to be.

These two examples illustrate how the science and the art of medicine can really come together and are a potent reminder that, ultimately, medicine is a job that involves working with human beings and needs its providers to be human too.

I recently sat in a team meeting which was so different and yet so similar to team meetings that have taken place over the past 25 years. The team I work with is one of the most committed and caring that I have ever worked with. Despite the pressures on us we still endeavour to provide a caring service that is child-centred in the simplest definition of the term.

Yet the days of straightforward or simple cases no longer exist. Many cases are with us because social care and education are underfunded too. There seems to be a constant game to pass the buck and label children as mentally ill when we are failing to provide them basic social and educational support. Policies appear to be more centred on ideology than on a child's best interests. The needs/wishes of parents still seem to be considered as more important than the needs of children. In the years I have practised there has been greater talk on children's needs but I am still not sure they are prioritised enough.

My own experiences of serious illness made me more patient-centred in my professional life, but not in the ways I had perhaps anticipated. I found that I became clearer about the need to avoid making assumptions about what an illness means to a patient. I had experienced so many assumptions made about me and what I must be feeling and thinking. Rarely did my experience reflect such assumptions, such as that having a huge scar on my leg would bother me. That actually was the least of my concerns!

I had also learnt that there is *no single right way of managing an illness*; there is no guidebook, and it is sometimes just about doing what feels right for yourself.

As a doctor, and especially as a psychiatrist, I have learnt to have no preconceived beliefs on whether the way people manage life events really says anything about them at all. I have also learnt through my own experience that making sense of experiences is such an individual and personal construct that I am not surprised to hear about the things that people do to get through. For example, I worked with a family who had 'worked around' their child's autism for nearly 16 years and so had come to see the boy's behaviour as him just being him. It was only through exploration that we were able to discover the symptomatology and behaviours they had accommodated as an extended family to manage the child.

We have a tendency to assume that certain life events inevitably lead to particular feelings or ways of being. When I reflect back over the past three decades and the knowledge I have gained, I conclude that, whatever commonalities may exist, we need to be open to the idea that each of us, including children, makes sense of the events in our lives in quite unique ways. Each person draws on a unique set of circumstances to come to terms with their experiences and the impact of these on their lives. The same principles can be applied to families and how they manage events and change.

Indeed, we can also learn from these principles in professional settings: all the things I have been asking patients to consider are now issues I need to consider with other members of my team. Managing the stress of working in the NHS is challenging and we are all coping in diverse ways, but not without considerable emotional cost.

There is certainly now greater awareness of children's mental health than when I began my career. The recognition needs to be better matched by appropriate funding and we need to ensure that children with mental health problems are treated by appropriately trained staff in the same way that children with physical health problems are. The research suggests that mental health problems in children and young people are rising – it is unclear whether this reflects better recognition or a true rise. It is likely to be a combination of both of these factors.

Perhaps the best way forward is to begin to teach young people to think about being mentally healthy in the same way that we talk about looking after physical health. The increased awareness of mental health should not perhaps just be about mental illness but also about promoting good mental health and trying to prevent mental illness. That requires us to see child mental health in a wider context and understand that social and political factors are as relevant today as they ever were. We need to enact this and value children in tangible ways by promoting their welfare and respecting their worth as children and not just future adults.

* * *

NISHA DOGRA is Professor of Psychiatry Education and an honorary consultant in child and adolescent psychiatry at the University of Leicester. Her clinical interests include working with adolescents, service improvement and development and audit. Her academic interests are training in psychiatry and diversity, for which she was awarded a University Teaching Fellowship. Nisha was a Commonwealth Fund Harkness Fellow in Health Care Policy in 2005–2006 and explored how different healthcare organisations implemented cultural competency training in various US contexts. In 2007 she was awarded a Health Foundation Leaders for Change Programme Award to implement service improvements. Nisha has published in the fields of medical education and child mental health, including six textbooks, several chapters in edited texts and over a hundred peer-reviewed articles.

7

Breaking the Silence and Secrecy of Childhood Sexual Abuse

CHRISTIANE SANDERSON

As a psychology undergraduate in the late 1980s I was struck by the deafening silence and secrecy faced by survivors of childhood sexual abuse (CSA). This was partly due to the shame and self-blame felt by many survivors and their fear of stigmatisation by others, including professionals such as therapists and social workers. When I proposed giving survivors a voice in my dissertation I was warned by my tutors that such research would not be considered to be psychologically robust and was better suited to the realm of social workers, not psychologists.

This was reinforced by staggeringly low estimated prevalence rates and a lack of clinical research into the lived experience of survivors apart from lone voices such as US sociologist David Finkelhor (1986), feminist writer and activist Diana Russell (1986), and poet Ellen Bass and author and abuse survivor Laura Davis, who collaborated in writing the self-help book *The Courage to Heal* (1988).

The past 30 years have seen a considerable shift in this estimate of prevalence rates as survivors have found the courage to speak out. This has been most powerfully demonstrated in survivors breaking the silence of CSA in institutions such as the church, boarding schools and children's homes, the scale of child exploitation within rings uncovered in English towns such as Rotherham, Rochdale and Oxford, as well as the prosecution of celebrities such as Jimmy Savile, Paul Gadd, Jonathan King and Ian Watkins.

These historical cases have highlighted the widespread prevalence of CSA, and how institutions and individuals have covered up sexual abuse by silencing victims and duping not only the child but also those in the child's social world – and in the case of Savile, duping a whole nation. This silencing of victims and survivors by perpetrators has all too often been compounded by professionals and authorities who have colluded through protecting perpetrators in covering up CSA or who have failed to believe victims, as happened following the sexual exploitation of children in communities such as Rotherham.

As survivors have acted to break the silence and secrecy of CSA, it's clear that they can no longer be ignored – their actions have resulted in a number of inquiries across the globe, including the UK where the Independent Inquiry into Childhood Sexual Abuse (IICSA) has been set up, and through which thousands of survivors will be able to give voice to their experiences.

Evidence on the extent of CSA in the past 30 years has also come from the proliferation of child sexual abuse images on the internet and cases in which perpetrators have used the internet to initiate child exploitation. As a result, awareness of CSA – its prevalence, impact and long-term effects – has increased alongside research in prevention and protection of children.

While this is commendable, what is often forgotten is the extent to which CSA occurs *in families*, which suggests that many children and survivors of CSA are still too afraid to disclose their abuse. Current research by the Children's Commissioner into CSA in families found in their 2015 report that 69 per cent of CSA occurs within the family (Children's Commissioner for England 2015), a finding that is echoed in the research by survivors' organisations such as One in Four (One in Four 2015) and Survivors in Transition (University Campus Suffolk and Survivors in Transition 2015). Current estimates of the prevalence of CSA – that one in four females and one in six males experience some form of CSA – may not reflect the full extent, and that there may be many more survivors who are still not able to speak out. We know, for example, that some particular areas of CSA remain under-reported, such as CSA by female perpetrators and by siblings.

While survivors are finally finding a voice and are being listened to and believed, they nevertheless still have difficulty accessing specialist service provision. Charities who specialise in supporting survivors of CSA remain woefully underfunded as they struggle with the number of survivors coming forward and with providing the longer-term counselling and therapy that many survivors of CSA require. All too often survivors of CSA are offered short-term counselling by generic counsellors who have little or no experience or specific training in working with CSA or sexual violence (One in Four 2015). This is despite increasing neurobiological evidence that CSA is a form of complex trauma that necessitates long-term therapeutic intervention (Herman 1992; Sanderson 2013; van der Kolk 2015).

The conceptualisation of CSA as trauma has led to a considerable change in treatment interventions. Since the inclusion of CSA in the Diagnostic and Statistical Manual of Mental Disorders (DSM-IV-TR) (American Psychiatric Association 2000) there has been increased recognition that the impact of CSA gives rise to a number of concomitant trauma reactions, which has enabled survivors to gain access to specialist services. However, it is clear that the current classification is insufficient to account for the range of symptoms seen in CSA and the need for a separate category of complex post-traumatic stress disorder (complex PTSD). While this was rejected for inclusion in DSM-5 (American Psychiatric Association 2013) it will be included in the eleventh revision of the International Classification of Diseases (ICD-11), to be published by the World Health Organization in 2018.

Conceptualising CSA as trauma has validated survivors' experiences and led to considerable research using neuroscience to improve understanding and develop evidence-based clinical interventions such as trauma-focused CBT (TfCBT) and eye movement desensitisation and reprocessing (EMDR). This has heightened the importance of using a trauma-focused model when working with survivors, where emphasis is placed on a phased approach through stabilisation, processing and integration. This ensures that the therapeutic process is paced in a more manageable way. In the first phase survivors are offered psychoeducation to help them understand their symptoms as normal reactions to trauma and learn how to manage these through emotional self-regulation and grounding skills. Once these skills have been mastered they are more able to tolerate distress, which allows them to move into phase two, in which the traumatic experiences are explored and processed. As survivors begin to make sense of their experiences they are able to move into phase three, in which the trauma becomes integrated, allowing them to reconnect to themselves and others, and promote post-traumatic growth (Sanderson 2013, 2016).

The conceptualisation of CSA as complex trauma has been of enormous benefit to survivors in validating their experiences and providing access to service provision. However, it is essential that current trauma-focused models not only try to heal the trauma but also combine this with rebuilding trust and 'relational worth'. By this, I mean the survivor's ability to reconnect with their self and others after the dehumanisation that accompanies CSA when the attachment system is hijacked – something which must be repaired through the therapeutic relationship. It is in giving a voice to the survivor and bearing witness to their abuse experiences that clinicians can help restore reality, diminish shame and facilitate post-traumatic growth. This takes time and is difficult to fully achieve in short-term therapy.

While many positive changes have occurred over the past 30 years in recognising and acknowledging the prevalence of CSA and the effects of trauma, there is a continuing need to listen to the lived experience of survivors in order to provide the optimal environment for them to recover and heal. The only way to protect children in the future and provide the best possible service to survivors is to make sure that they are given a voice, and are listened to and believed.

Victims and survivors need to know that they will no longer be silenced or betrayed. Professionals and clinicians can no longer remain silent, and must speak out to ensure that all victims and survivors are given access to the counselling they need and are fully supported in their healing.

References

American Psychiatric Association (2000) *Diagnostic and Statistical Manual of Mental Disorders, DSM-IV-TR*. Washington, DC: American Psychiatric Association.

American Psychiatric Association (2013) *Diagnostic and Statistical Manual of Mental Disorders, 5th Edition: DSM-5*. Washington, DC: American Psychiatric Association.

Bass, E. and Davis, L. (1988) *The Courage to Heal: A Guide for Women Survivors of Child Sexual Abuse*. Bloomington, IN: Collins Living.

Children's Commissioner for England (2015) *Protecting Children from Harm: A Critical Assessment of Child Sexual Abuse in the Family Network in England and Priorities for Action*. London: Office of the Children's Commissioner for England.

Finkelhor, D. (1986) *Sourcebook on Child Sexual Abuse*. New York: Sage.

Herman, J. (1992) *Trauma and Recovery: The Aftermath of Violence*. New York: Basic Books.

One in Four (2015) *Survivors' Voices*. London: One in Four.

Russell, D. E. H. (1986) *The Secret Trauma: Incest in the Lives of Girls and Women*. New York: Basic Books.

Sanderson, C. (2013) *Counselling Skills for Working with Trauma: Healing from Child Sexual Abuse, Sexual Violence and Domestic Abuse* (Essential Skills for Counselling). London: Jessica Kingsley Publishers.

Sanderson, C. (2016) *The Warrior Within: A One in Four Handbook to Aid Recovery from Childhood Sexual Abuse and Violence*, third edition. London: One in Four.

University Campus Suffolk and Survivors in Transition (2015) *Hear Me. Believe Me. Respect Me. Focus on Survivors: A Survey of Adult Survivors of Childhood Sexual Abuse and Their Experiences of Support Services*. Ipswich: University Campus Suffolk and Survivors in Transition. www.uos.ac.uk/sites/default/files/basic_file/Focus-on-Survivors-Final-Copy-Logo-Blk.pdf (accessed 27 July 2017).

van der Kolk, B. A. (2015) *The Body Keeps the Score*. London: Penguin.

* * *

CHRISTIANE SANDERSON, BSc, MSc, is a senior lecturer in psychology at the University of Roehampton with 30 years' experience of working with survivors of child sexual abuse, sexual violence, complex trauma and domestic abuse. She is the author of numerous books, including *Counselling Skills for Working with Shame* (2015), *Counselling*

Skills for Working with Trauma: Healing from Child Sexual Abuse, Sexual Violence and Domestic Abuse (2013) and *Counselling Adult Survivors of Child Sexual Abuse*, third edition (2006), all published by Jessica Kingsley Publishers. She has also written *Responding to Survivors of Child Sexual Abuse: A Pocket Guide for Professionals, Partners, Families and Friends* (2015), *The Warrior Within: A One in Four Handbook to Aid Recovery from Childhood Sexual Abuse and Violence* (2013) and *The Spirit Within: A One in Four Handbook to Aid Recovery from Religious Sexual Abuse Across All Faiths* (2011), all published by the charity One in Four, for whom she is a trustee, and provided the analysis for the One in Four report *Survivors' Voices: Breaking the Silence* (2015) on living with the impact of child sexual abuse in the family environment.

8

Dementia

Reflections, 1987–2017

DAWN BROOKER

The field of dementia care has changed beyond recognition in the past 30 years. In part, this has been driven by the sheer numbers of people whose lives are now affected by dementia. The number of people aged 75 and over has increased by 84 per cent over this period (Office for National Statistics 2015). This means that the numbers of people surviving into the age range in which dementia most commonly occurs has grown in real terms. In 1987, dementia was barely spoken about in its own right and was seen as an insignificant part of older people's psychiatric care. A report published by the Health Advisory Service called *The Rising Tide: Developing Services for Mental Illness in Old Age* was published in 1982 and was a report that I remember reading with great interest. This highlighted the rising numbers of people we should expect to develop dementia and called for 'joint planning and provision of comprehensive services for the elderly mentally ill'. The predictions they made about the numbers came true.

The number of people with dementia in the UK is forecast to increase to over 1 million by 2025 and over 2 million by 2051. There are over 40,000 people with early-onset dementia (under 65) in the UK. Dementia impacts on the whole family and society. A survey by Alzheimer's Research UK (2015) showed that 24.6 million people had a close family member or friend living with dementia. Unfortunately, the strenuous suggestions the Health Advisory Service made about joined-up comprehensive services to meet these growing needs have not yet materialised.

In 1987 I was working as the lead clinical psychologist in the NHS services for older people in Birmingham. Even the language then was radically different. My job title was the EMI (elderly mentally infirm) clinical psychologist. My office was in a psychiatric hospital (the asylum) covering many long-stay wards which were mainly populated by elderly people. Some had lived almost all of their lives in hospital, having been admitted for being pregnant out of wedlock or for some other 'misdemeanour'. Many patients who I saw in those early days had undergone hundreds of electric convulsive therapy treatments and brain surgery, and prescribed mind-bending drugs. There was little formal diagnosis of dementia. People were generally classified as 'senile'. The ward that catered for people with advanced dementia and physical health problems was known as the 'babies ward' by the nursing staff and known as the 'non-ambulant dements ward' in official documents.

This was 1987, not Victorian England.

My grandfather had dementia, although it was never called that of course. Pre-school, he was my constant companion. He had lots of love and time to spend on a boisterous but lonely little girl. He always called me Joan (my mum's name) and would play endless rounds of 'Pat a cake, pat a cake'. I loved him. When he died suddenly (probably of pneumonia I think now) all my aunties said it was a blessing – him being how he was. They obviously did not know how nice our life was! I was furious with them.

I have carried that sense of injustice with me for a long time and I know that many others who found themselves working in health and social care in the 1980s shared it. As a psychologist, however, I lacked any real theory to understand the needs of the people with advanced dementia. There were very few books, and even fewer journals, that carried anything of substance on dementia care. The emotional and psychological needs of people living with dementia simply were not considered. The overarching rhetoric was that dementia was the death that left the body behind and people were just an empty shell.

In 1988 I heard a then-unknown academic called Tom Kitwood speak at our annual Psychology Special Interest Group Conference. He spoke of malignant social psychology and dialectics of dementia. These were heady concepts for a jobbing clinician but at last I had a set of psychological theories that helped me to understand the emotions and behaviour of people living with dementia. This empowered me to recognise that there was a lot that could be done through improving our empathy and communication to improve the quality of people's lives. It was as if someone had shone a bright light on the lives of the people that I worked with day in, day out. Many working in the field heard Tom's words and consumed a series of journal articles he produced over the next ten years, culminating in his book *Dementia Reconsidered: The Person Comes First* in 1997 (Kitwood 1997). We saw for the first time what we could do to help people.

By 1993, I was still working in the NHS but I was much more focused on shaping services as a whole to actually support people psychologically. I was now employed as the quality assurance manager for the newly named Mental Health Services for Older Adults in Birmingham. Tom Kitwood trained 50 of our staff in the brand new person-centred tool called Dementia Care Mapping and we instituted an extensive person-centred quality improvement programme.

We closed the old asylum and safely moved patients into community units utilising external advocacy services for all long-stay patients. Some had been in hospital for over 50 years. We had Community Mental Health Teams who worked directly with all the care homes in the city, which were then run by local authorities rather than for profit. There was no concern about who was paying for care and whether care was medical or social. Our NHS community-based multi-disciplinary teams undertook assessment and treatment in people's own homes in recognition that we needed to keep people out of hospital. There was fully integrated working between health and social services, and I married a social worker to prove it!

We were full of hope for the future of community care. We thought that malignant social psychology would be eradicated along with the long-stay wards. The drug donepezil was licensed for the symptomatic treatment of the Alzheimer's type of dementia in the mid-1990s. This meant that the medical profession and pharmaceutical companies now had a clear role in the diagnosis and management of dementia. There was at last a hope that we would find a cure for dementia.

Unfortunately, milk and honey were not just around the corner for people with dementia and their families.

The market economy of care and the lack of dementia expertise in regulation and commissioning that mushroomed in its wake, the over-medicalisation of dementia, institutional ageism, the assumption that therapy and rehabilitation were wasted on people with dementia, targets, lack of professional accountability and asset stripping of services all took their toll. A particular low point was illustrated in the 'noughties' with the terrible situation at the Mid Staffordshire NHS Trust as outlined in the Francis Report in 2013 (Francis 2013). Patients and their families endured terrible and shocking mistreatment for years in an NHS that was obsessed by financial targets and only reporting 'good' news. The cure for dementia was not just around the corner. Many millions have been spent but no magic bullet has yet materialised.

By far the biggest blessing today is that people living with dementia are now speaking out with their own voices rather than being hidden away and treated as if they have nothing to say. My friend, the late Peter Ashley, was one of the innovators in this country to speak out publicly about his experience of living with dementia. He, and others who have followed, have captivated the public, professionals and politicians to help us all to better understand the emotional impact of life with dementia. He said, 'I'm not dying with dementia, I'm living with dementia.'

He and many others worldwide have broken the stereotype of what someone with dementia is 'supposed' to be like. Having people who can talk directly from their experience is so important in combating stigma and fear. It helps all of us not to fear the future so much. Their voices have led to the National Dementia Strategy, Dementia Action Alliance, PM Challenges and Dementia Friends initiatives. Dementia is spoken about at G7 events, the

OECD, the World Health Organization and the United Nations. We have books, research and journals on areas of care and support that we never dreamt were possible 30 years ago. We have lots of evidence and knowledge about how to provide skilled person-centred care, support and assistance but there is still a disconnection about getting this into regular practice. It is a global challenge and it demands a global response – in the same way that we need a global response to find a cure for dementia.

The need for person-centred care will not be eliminated even if we find a good pharmaceutical solution. The process of being diagnosed and being treated requires high standards of care, now and into the future.

References

Alzheimer's Research UK (2015) *Dementia in the Family: The Impact on Carers.* www.alzheimersresearchuk.org/wp-content/uploads/2015/12/Dementia-in-the-Family-The-impact-on-carers.pdf (accessed 15 August 2017).

Francis, R. (Chair) (2013) *Report of the Mid Staffordshire NHS Foundation Trust Public Inquiry: Executive Summary.* London: The Stationery Office.

Health Advisory Service (1982) *The Rising Tide: Developing Services for Mental Illness in Old Age.* London: Health Advisory Service.

Kitwood, T. (1997) *Dementia Reconsidered: The Person Comes First.* Buckingham: Open University Press.

Office for National Statistics (2015) 'Population Estimates for UK, England and Wales, Scotland and Northern Ireland, Mid-2014.' http://webarchive. nationalarchives.gov.uk/20160105165857/http://www.ons.gov.uk/ons/rel/ pop-estimate/population-estimates-for-uk--england-and-wales--scotland-and-northern-ireland/mid-2014/index.html (accessed 15 September 2017).

* * *

DAWN BROOKER is the Director of the Association for Dementia Studies at the University of Worcester where she leads a multi-disciplinary team dedicated to improving the lives of those living with dementia through research, education and practice development. She qualified as a clinical psychologist in 1984 and her academic work is grounded in practice experience gained from a variety of NHS clinical and leadership roles in services for older people dating back to this time. She is internationally recognised for scholarship in practice development of person-centred dementia care and has long-established working relationships with practitioners and scholars worldwide. Professor Brooker enjoys working at the interface between the experience of those living with dementia, those developing care practice and those undertaking research to ensure that there is real knowledge transfer and translation between these different world-views.

9

A Brief Story of Counselling in Schools Since 1987

NICK LUXMOORE

I began work as a secondary school counsellor in January 1987, the same year that Jessica Kingsley Publishers opened its doors. At the time, school counsellors were the exception rather than the rule in the UK. The school I joined had never had one before, but the headteacher had worked with a counsellor elsewhere and had persuaded his governors to fund this new half-time appointment.

Although I'd started training as a psychotherapist, I'd only actually trained as a counsellor for a year and – then as now – most counselling training was geared towards working with adults rather than young people. I was lucky, however, to have been a teacher for several years already, and so understood something about young people and about the way schools work. Without that experience, I'd have been lost. (The headteacher left the school almost as soon as I arrived!)

Things have moved on during the past 30 years. Nationally, school counsellors have a much higher profile.

There is counselling provision of some sort in 80 per cent of all English and Scottish secondary schools. In Wales and in Northern Ireland local authorities are obliged to provide a counselling service for every secondary school.

This growth of counselling in schools has been matched by a decline in the pastoral time allocated to teachers. Schools still believe in producing well-rounded, happy, confident individuals, but the reality is that teachers are currently judged by their ability to deliver an academic curriculum. Their jobs and the status of their school depend on exam results, where good exam results attract more students to the school, and more students attract more money. So, time spent listening to the distress of students tends to get squeezed in the course of a busy day, especially if teachers themselves are distressed at the impossibility of their jobs. At this point, counsellors and other often badly paid, often part-time members of staff are sent in to mop up the mess!

The way these 'emotional caretakers' operate is as varied now as it was in 1987, partly because there are different 'modalities' in counselling, just as in religion where there are different faiths and different ways of expressing a faith. The comparison with religion is deliberate because counsellors sometimes cling to their particular modality as if it is a religious faith! At one extreme, there are person-centred counsellors, tracing their descent back to Carl Rogers. At the other extreme there are psychodynamic counsellors with an allegiance to Freud and his successors. There are 'integrative' counsellors, trying to hold a middle ground, and there are other counsellors identifying themselves variously with cognitive behaviour therapy, solution-focused therapy, transactional analysis, gestalt therapy and an increasing number of newer modalities, all of them competing (in the nicest possible way) for supremacy. Pity the poor headteacher going through the job applications, trying to understand the jargon!

Over the years, I've helped various headteachers with this. 'What exactly should we be looking for?' they ask. 'Is there a typical job description? What salary should we be offering? How involved in school life should we expect our counsellor to be?' Some avoid these questions by hiring an outside agency to supply a counsellor who simply comes into the school, sees individuals and goes away again. This is often cheaper for the school and suits schools wanting to keep counselling at arm's length in the name of confidentiality and privacy. It also suits a small minority of schools where the need for counselling is still regarded as shameful. However, it doesn't suit those schools looking for a more integrated service where, potentially, the counsellor will be providing a service to members of staff as well as to students and will be involved in all sorts of other initiatives: running schemes where students are trained and supervised to support each other, training staff, working with parents, liaising with outside agencies and looking to have an effect on the whole culture of the school.

Some headteachers will say that they'd like to have their school to have its own counsellor and they'd like that person to be integrated into school life, but that budget cuts mean there can only be a skeleton service. It's true that governments have reduced, increased and then reduced school budgets during the past 30 years. Headteachers have sometimes struggled to put teachers in front of classes, never mind pay for a shiny new counsellor. And yet in 2017 there are more counsellors in UK schools than ever before.

One reason for this is that, during the past 30 years, counsellors have got their act together. On the whole, they're now better trained than before (or better able to adapt their training). They understand the importance of keeping a public profile in their school. The British Association of Counselling and Psychotherapy (BACP), with its dedicated *Children & Young People* journal, has campaigned hard to get counselling into more schools and has been effective as an umbrella organisation for counsellors, allowing experiences to be shared and lessons learned. Research continues to make the case for counselling in schools, not least because we now know that most mental illnesses have begun by the time young people leave school. Neuroscience has shown that brains develop through human relationships, and that children in happy relationships are therefore likely to learn more effectively, producing better exam results.

Over the past 30 years, a lot of work has gone into de-stigmatising mental illness and counselling, and into helping schools to understand more about the internal worlds of young people. Once, school counsellors worried about glue sniffing, fighting, HIV, unplanned pregnancies and unemployment. Now they worry about anxiety, self-harm, depression and suicide. Of course schools still long for quick fixes and for concrete evidence of the effectiveness of counselling, and of course there are still charlatans peddling miracle cures.

Complacency would be foolish. But significant progress has been made, and Jessica Kingsley Publishers has contributed to this, helping to disseminate ideas in so many fields.

* * *

NICK LUXMOORE has worked with students and staff in schools for 40 years as a counsellor, teacher, youth worker and United Kingdom Council for Psychotherapy (UKCP) registered psychotherapist. He has published ten books including *School Counsellors Working with Young People and Staff: A Whole-School Approach* (Jessica Kingsley Publishers, 2014) and *Essential Listening Skills for Busy School Staff* (Jessica Kingsley Publishers, 2015).

10

Reflections on the Past 30 Years of Restorative Practice in the UK

BELINDA HOPKINS

Back in 1987 the phrase 'restorative justice' had been around for about ten years but was not widely known.[1] I certainly was not to come across it for another eight or so years. However, the core values and principles I would later identify as 'restorative' were not only known to me, but already ones I held dear in my approach to teaching: namely the importance of mutual respect between human beings; the importance of giving everyone a voice in matters that concern them; and collaborative problem-solving.

---

1 The term 'restorative justice' was first coined by Albert Eglash in 1977 (Van Ness and Heetderks Strong 2010). He distinguished between three approaches to justice:
   - 'retributive justice', based on punishment
   - 'distributive justice', involving therapeutic treatment of offenders
   - 'restorative justice', based on restitution with input from victims and offenders.

Right from the beginning of my teaching career in the early 1980s I had been influenced by the writings of Paolo Freire (1970), John Holt (1966) and Everett Reimer (1971), all of whom were critical of mainstream educational ideas and of the suppression of children's creativity, autonomy and voice. My early experiments with democratic problem-solving in the classroom put me at odds with fellow teachers.

By 1990 I had two very young children and was soon learning the art of conflict resolution first-hand. The book *How to Talk so Kids Will Listen and Listen so Kids Will Talk* (Faber and Mazlish 1980) was an early 'parenting bible' for me and I still recommend it today on my courses.

After a few years at home I returned to teaching. I soon found that once again my values and beliefs about what teaching should be about were at odds with what I was expected to do and say when things went wrong in the classroom. Like the vast majority of teachers, I had received little, if any, training in so-called 'behaviour management'. I sought help in further training. The course Playing with Fire (Macbeth and Fine 2011) at LEAP Confronting Conflict, a national charity that provides conflict management training and support to young people and professionals, was a Damascus Road experience for me. What I learned on the course was so inspiring, I realised for the first time what I wanted to do in my life: share the skills of community-building, conflict resolution and mediation to as many students and staff as I could. I began offering regular 'circle time' to classes and practised mediation at the school when students fell out.

I experienced the power of regular circle work,[2] and saw how it can develop emotional literacy and give everyone in the circle a voice and an opportunity to share their thoughts, feelings and needs. I saw how it empowered children to be problem-solvers, and build empathy and compassion. I saw evidence of how behavioural issues and conflicts between class members were much diminished by having regular circle experiences with each other. I began to teach more and more of my modern language classes using the circle time format, with very positive results both academically and socially among the students. And I knew that I wanted to share all these discoveries more widely than in one school. With a huge leap of faith and much encouragement from my husband, by 1994 I had left the classroom and established myself as a freelance conflict resolution trainer, and my company Transforming Conflict was born. I also became involved in neighbourhood mediation as a volunteer and subsequently a trainer of these skills, helping in setting up several local mediation services.

And so it was that in the mid-1990s I was in the right place at the right time when Thames Valley Police began to take an interest in something called 'restorative justice'. At first I was not aware of what it was, but was lucky enough to be funded by them to introduce a peer mediation service into a primary school. The service, in Geoffrey Field Junior School in South Reading, is still running today.

This early involvement was probably why I was invited to hear Australian police officer Terry O'Connell speak to a gathering of police, probation, youth justice and local authority professionals in the mid-1990s, and why I was

---

2   Circle work is time spent with others sitting in a circle, using a talking piece to indicate who has the opportunity to speak and taking it in turns around the circle to contribute.

then invited to train as a restorative justice conference facilitator and join the training team to roll the practice out across police services nationwide. I was also invited by the Thames Valley Police Restorative Justice Consultancy to join with others to think about how restorative justice could be used in schools.

The late 1990s and early 2000s were a heady time to be working in the Thames Valley and be involved in the field of restorative justice. I worked closely with Thames Valley Police Restorative Justice Consultancy and the Thames Valley Partnership, and had many opportunities to be among the pioneers and early adopters who have helped lay down the foundations of the restorative justice policies that are in place today.

Between 1997 and 2007 I began to read as much as I could and was inspired by writers like Howard Zehr and Harry Mika (Zehr 1990; Zehr and Mika 1997), American criminologists considered to be pioneers of the modern concept of restorative justice. I wrote about the links between restorative justice in criminal settings and in school settings, and about the links to fields I already knew well – conflict resolution, mediation and circle time. At first what I wrote was unpublished and simply shared with colleagues in the field, but I was increasingly asked to speak at conferences and events, planting very early seeds of interest. I went on to offer courses to trainee and practising teachers, and to study for a PhD researching the impact of training in restorative skills on teachers. This was in 2000, at a time when the widespread use of restorative practice in schools did not yet exist, but as I explain below, the passage of time during which the thesis was written also served to chart the rise in real time of restorative practice.

The PhD comprised a series of case studies. The first was on the first state school to have received training in restorative conferencing.[3] By the time I came to start the second case study, I had developed a course especially for teachers which moved beyond the high-end practice of conferencing and introduced informal skills for day-to-day encounters. This course was commissioned by Thames Valley Police, and trialled on some Oxfordshire Pupil Referral Unit staff. I was then invited to train some staff at an Oxfordshire secondary school and representatives from some of their feeder primary schools. This initiative – the first of its kind in the UK – became my second case study.

By the time I was ready for a third case study the field had developed even further. A visionary educational psychologist, Brian Steel, and the head of an inclusion unit[4] in North Lanarkshire, Agnes Donnelly, had by now heard of restorative justice in schools. Having visited the pioneering projects being developed in Pennsylvania by Ted and Susan Wachtel (who went on to found the International Institute for Restorative Justice, one of the largest providers of training in restorative practice in the world), they were keen to roll out the approach across all North Lanarkshire schools. I was invited to train all the primary headteachers in the county – a job I did with my now growing team of trainers. As luck would have it, very soon after this was arranged, the Scottish Education Minister decided he wanted restorative justice to be introduced into all Scottish schools. He funded a pilot

---

3   Restorative conferencing describes a meeting facilitated by a restorative practitioner following extensive preparation with all individuals involved to ensure everyone is willing to participate. Key features of the meeting include who participates, the seating arrangements and the facilitation style.

4   An inclusion unit is a place where those excluded from school for whatever reason are provided with education and support.

in three counties – North Lanarkshire, Fife and Highlands. This initiative has since been evaluated by academics from Edinburgh and Glasgow universities (Lloyd *et al.* 2007).

As if I was not busy enough at this heady time, my desire to capture my ideas and my vision in book form grew. Fortunately this coincided with Jessica Kingsley Publishers developing an interest in the field, having published previously on mediation, and I am grateful to Marian Liebmann for recommending me and my work to JKP. This was how *Just Schools* (Hopkins 2004) came to be written: the first book of its kind in Europe and, I am proud to say, still hailed as one of the 'bibles' in the subject by many worldwide.

Unbeknown to me, Marg Thorsborne, a trainer and practitioner in Australia who had worked closely with Terry O'Connell, was developing her own ideas along similar lines and had published a book about schools a year or so earlier. Marg and I met at one of the inspiring Winchester Restorative Justice conferences[5] and we have been admirers of each other's work ever since. Now Marg is also a JKP author and has written some of JKP's most popular books on aspects of restorative practice in schools (Thorsborne and Blood 2013; Kelly and Thorsborne 2014; Burnett and Thorsborne 2015).

The field of restorative justice continued to develop apace in the late 2000s. Interest in schools grew, as did growing interest in using a restorative approach in residential care homes for children. Hertfordshire was the first county to train all their residential care staff in restorative conferencing, and I drew on my training to adapt the principles outlined

---

5   A series of innovative and exciting international conferences promoting restorative justice were held in the mid-2000s in Winchester. I was on the organizing committee for this conference for several years.

in *Just Schools* for a further book on residential care, *Just Care* (Hopkins 2009), which was shaped by feedback from those practitioners in Hertfordshire on what they needed. It was the first book to help people implement a restorative culture across a residential home, and has also been used to train foster carers.

The past ten years has seen the field of restorative practice develop beyond recognition from those early pioneering days. The Ministry of Justice is now firmly behind the use of restorative justice in the criminal justice system and there are hubs and services all over the UK. All youth offending services have expertise in this area. There is still a long way to go, but restorative justice has become increasingly mainstream.

We have a national umbrella body called the Restorative Justice Council (RJC) which continues to develop quality standards and accreditation. I am proud to have been working with them, as a board member and subsequently on various advisory bodies developing the Principles of Restorative Justice, National Practice Standards and the various forms of accreditation and quality marks now available for individual as well as organisational practice (Restorative Justice Consortium 2005; Restorative Justice Council 2015).

Sadly I cannot report a growing support of the work by the Department for Education where, if anything, recommended policies are at odds with the values and principles of restorative practice (see, for example, Bennett 2017). However, Ofsted is now increasingly acknowledging the role of restorative practice in helping establish safe and caring schools, and encouraging young people to think more about how to behave with each other and with staff. The lack of top-level governmental support across the UK is in stark contrast to the financial support the Ministry of Justice is willing to provide for a range of restorative initiatives in the criminal justice field.

However, there are more and more schools across the UK aspiring to implement restorative practice at some level, and some even want to transform the whole culture of the school, using restorative principles and practices across the whole school community.

Restorative practice does not have a monopoly on emotional literacy, community building, social justice, the empowerment of those with less-heard voices, conflict resolution, mediation and community problem-solving. However, it has gradually come to embrace all these elements as part of a wider restorative practice jigsaw puzzle. All of these practices flow naturally from restorative values, principles and practice, and looking back to those early days of the 1980s I now know I was a 'restorative' teacher then without realising it.

People have come to realise that restorative values, principles and practice have applicability in all sorts of fields beyond criminal and youth justice – not just education and residential care but also in social care more widely: with hard-to-reach young people and their families, or those with no families living in sheltered accommodation; in prisons and young offenders institutions; in healthcare; in community work; and indeed in business and other workplace settings.

I feel sure that the next decade will bring further innovation and culture transformation in such settings. Indeed, there are already increasingly common debates about what a restorative institution, organisation, company or workplace might look like, and about how to become a restorative town, city or county. A few places use these terms already – although I think in some cases these may be more aspirational than a reflection of reality.

Having said that, there is nothing wrong with having a vision or aspirations to change the world. It is what gets me out of bed in the morning, even now, after 30 years or more of striving to make a difference to the lives of children, young people and the adults who work with them. I enjoy sharing my experience with newer and younger advocates for restorative practice.

It is curious to have become one of the 'elders' in the field, but I am proud to have played my part and I still have more I want to achieve. My recent edited book *Restorative Theory in Practice* (Hopkins 2016) was a wonderful opportunity to encourage new people to put their wisdom and expertise down in words. I would like to do more of this kind of collaborative venture – for me it epitomises restorative practice.

References

Bennett, T. (2017) 'Creating a Culture: How school leaders can optimise behaviour. Independent review of behaviour in schools.' https://www.gov.uk/government/uploads/system/uploads/attachment_data/file/602487/Tom_Bennett_Independent_Review_of_Behaviour_in_Schools.pdf (accessed 15 September 2017).

Burnett, N. and Thorsborne, M. (2015) *Restorative Practice and Special Needs*. New York: Rawson, Wade Publishers

Faber, J. and Mazlish, E. (1980) *How to Talk so Kids Will Listen and Listen so Kids Will Talk*. London: Piccadilly Press.

Freire, P. (1970) *Pedagogy of the Oppressed*. New York: Seabury Press

Holt, J. (1966) *How Children Fail*. London: Pitman

Hopkins, B. (2004) *Just Schools: A Whole School Approach to Restorative Justice*. London: Jessica Kingsley Publishers.

Hopkins, B. (2009) *Just Care: Restorative Justice Approaches to Working with Children in Public Care*. London: Jessica Kingsley Publishers.

Hopkins, B. (ed.) (2016) *Restorative Theory in Practice*. London: Jessica Kingsley Publishers.

Kelly, V. and Thorsborne, M. (eds) (2014) *The Psychology of Emotion in Restorative Practice.* London: Jessica Kingsley Publishers.

Lloyd, G., McCluskey, G., Riddell, S., Stead, J., Weedon, E. and Kane, J. (2007) 'Restorative Practices in three Scottish Councils: Evaluation of pilot projects 2004–2006: Executive Summary. Edinburgh: Scottish Executive.' www.gov.scot/Resource/Doc/195982/0052537.pdf (accessed 15 September 2017).

Macbeth, F. and Fine, N. (2011) *Playing with Fire: Training for Those Working with Young People in Conflict*, second edition. London: Jessica Kingsley Publishers.

Reimer, E. (1971) *School is Dead.* London: Penguin

Restorative Justice Consortium (2005) 'Statement of Restorative Justice Principles as applied in a school setting, second edition.' https://restorativejustice.org.uk/sites/default/files/files/Principles%20in%20schools.pdf (accessed 15 September 2017).

Restorative Justice Council (2015) 'Principles of restorative practice.' https://restorativejustice.org.uk/resources/rjc-principles-restorative-practice (accessed 15 September 2017).

Thorsborne, M. and Blood, P. (2013) *Implementing Restorative Practice in Schools.* London: Jessica Kingsley Publishers

Van Ness, D.W. and Heetderks Strong, K. (2010) *Restoring Justice: An Introduction to Restorative Justice*, fourth edition. New Province, NJ: Matthew Bender & Co., Inc.

Zehr, H. (1990) *Changing Lenses.* Scottdale, PA: Herald Press.

Zehr, H. and Mika, H. (1997) *Fundamental Concepts of Restorative Justice.* Mennonite Central Committee http://www.cehd.umn.edu/ssw/RJP/Projects/Victim-Offender-Dialogue/RJ_Principles/Fundamental_Concepts_RJ_Zehr_Mika.PDF (accessed 15 September 2017)

* * *

BELINDA HOPKINS has been pioneering restorative approaches in youth settings across the UK and beyond for over 20 years. In the early 1990s she founded Transforming Conflict and this organisation has established itself as one of the foremost providers of training and consultancy in the field of restorative approaches nationally and internationally. The organisation has been recognised as a provider of high quality training by the UK's Restorative Justice Council (RJC).

Belinda gained her doctorate in 2006 with research into the implementation of a whole-school restorative approach. She is passionate about sharing how the ethos, principles and practices of restorative approaches can transform communities and institutions.

She still runs training courses herself, writes books and articles, develops training materials and resources, and speaks at conferences nationally and internationally. Belinda currently sits on the Restorative Justice Council's Expert Advisory Group and is an RJC-accredited practitioner. She continues to keep her own restorative practice up to scratch by volunteering for a local RJ service working with victims and offenders.

11

Youth Work

Personal, Social and Political Education

VANESSA ROGERS

Youth workers today are part of a rich history of work with young people stretching back to the late nineteenth century. From the early pioneers responding to fears about young people moving away from rural villages and into the big cities to earn a wage in the factories of the industrial revolution, to more recent government policies on antisocial behaviour and teenage pregnancy, the core issues arguably remain the same.

The Youth Work National Occupational Standards (National Youth Agency 2012) state that the key purpose of youth work is to 'enable young people to develop holistically, working with them to facilitate their personal, social and educational development, to enable them to develop their voice, influence and place in society and to reach their full potential' (p.4). This formal definition of 'youth work' is helpful in identifying what differentiates youth workers from other professionals working with young people, but what does it mean in practice?

For me, what's missing in this definition of youth work is the word 'political'. Historically, youth work did not develop just to keep young people off the streets or to provide aimless amusement (Smith 2013); it has always offered personal, social and political education in an informal environment: the politics of being a young person, the politics of being an active citizen, the political that *is* personal.

Anyone who has a teenager or has been a teenager can tell you it's not always easy. While we live in a society that applauds looking as youthful as possible for as long as possible, not many people are so keen on the more tumultuous parts of growing up. Who would willingly go back to the self-conscious angst and heartbreak of first love? The constant worry about being normal, fitting in and being acceptable to peers? Or the stress induced by exams and the need to make big decisions that seemingly affect the rest of your life?

I would wager that many adults don't remember this bit when they gaze back at their youth through rose-tinted glasses. Yes, you may have been able to eat chocolate and still have a flat stomach, but what about all of the worries about spots, blackheads and break-outs, usually about the time of those important first dates? I cannot be alone in remembering my dismay at a rapidly changing body that seemed for the most part out of my control.

Alongside all the biological changes, adolescence is a time of turbulence as teenagers struggle to find out who they are and take risks as they kick the edges of acceptable to find the boundaries. Good youth work may look as if it just 'happens', but the success of it actually depends on careful planning, clear aims and measurable outcomes. The youth work curriculum includes sex and relationships, mental health and emotional wellbeing, as well as life skills, online safety and citizenship to reflect the different aspects of growing up in the UK today. From learning how to cook to learning how to vote, effective youth work creates an environment where young people can safely discuss their feelings, hopes and dreams, as well as ask questions about the things that are important to them, without the fear of being 'judged'.

But this is not without its challenges. By encouraging young people to talk openly about their opinions, youth workers can be faced with a wide range of views, some of which may at best conflict with their own and at worst be offensive or even illegal. Youth work teaches that everyone has a right to a voice, and it is that right we struggle to uphold, rather than blindly agreeing to respect all views. This is how youth work can effectively challenge emotive issues like discrimination and prejudice, not just by educating young people about the law, but by creating a safe place to hold alternative views up to the light and examine where they come from, questioning and offering different perspectives and providing young people with opportunities to try out different ways of being or thinking. Simply accusing someone of wrong thinking if you don't like what they say is not likely to change their mind; rather it reinforces, shuts the conversation down and deepens the divide between 'us' and 'them'.

More importantly, young people are not always wrong and inexperience does not necessarily equate to ignorance. As a youth worker I have listened to young people express outrage, anger and dismay as they question the world around them: a world that many feel has failed them in terms of education, employment opportunities and the ability to eventually afford their own home within their local community. They are not wrong to share these concerns, and their sense of grievance is understandable.

Young people can be innovative and visionary, with energy and enthusiasm to shape and change the world. To do this they need to find ways to get their voices heard and be able to see that their participation in things like youth councils, forums and consultations actually makes a difference. Good examples of this are young people joining the debate over whether Britain should leave the EU in 2016 and the impact of the youth vote in the general election of 2017, both provoking passionate debates on both sides of the argument, and a demand to know what is going to happen as a consequence of the voting. Using the tools these young people grew up with in this digital age, a peaceful but powerful protest can be shared with millions via social media.

Put simply, providing young people with a 'good time' is not enough to qualify as 'youth work'. To pass muster, youth work must offer young people the opportunity to meet, socialise, develop new skills and learn to question and challenge what they see both locally and globally. Detached projects should not be about forcing young people off the streets and away from adult eyes, but more about building trust and developing interesting projects that meet needs and reflect local issues. Essentially, we all share the same living space, so why not invest in young people through youth work so that we can make it a safer, healthier and more positive experience for everyone?

References

National Youth Agency (2012) *LS1 YW00 Youth Work National Occupational Standards*. www.nya.org.uk/wp-content/uploads/2014/06/National-Occupation-Standards-for-Youth-Work.pdf (accessed 4 August 2017).

Smith, M. K. (2013) 'What is youth work? Exploring the history, theory and practice of work with young people.' Infed: The Encyclopedia of Informal Education. www.infed.org/mobi/what-is-youth-work-exploring-the-history-theory-and-practice-of-work-with-young-people (accessed 2 August 2017).

* * *

VANESSA ROGERS is a nationally acclaimed youth work consultant and trainer with experience of managing a wide range of services for young people (11–25), including early intervention and targeted services. She is best known for creating practical, easy-to-follow educational resources, enabling practitioners to engage teenagers in learning about even the most emotive of topics, including sex, drugs and pornography. She continues to work with young people across the UK on a commissioned basis, is a fellow of the Royal Society of Arts (RSA) and sits on the council for the Institute for Youth Work (IYW).

12

Children's Rights and Power

PRISCILLA ALDERSON

During the 1990s, Professor Mary John at Exeter University started the 'Children in Charge' series for Jessica Kingsley Publishers. The series took children's own views and experiences very seriously, from Cathy Kiddle's (1999) book on traveller children to Rhys Griffith (1998) on young students' critical perspectives of secondary school.

Mary's book *Children's Rights and Power* (2003) moved beyond the usual '3Ps' – protection, provision and participation rights – to the key but too often neglected fourth P – power. The book examined vital ways in which power is central to rights, and people of all ages become powerful through their responses to risk and challenge, as Mary observed in the Free School in Albany, US, with child workers in Mexico, and at the Barefoot College in Rajasthan, where working children organised their own evening schools and parliament.

After Mary invited me to write *Young Children's Rights* (2008) for the series, colleagues from around the world sent examples of young children aged up to eight years of age exercising their rights. My book examines the question:

If 'human rights' really mean 'human' and apply to every human being, how do they relate to the youngest children and babies? Far too often, 'human' is assumed to mean 'fully human and therefore adult' as if young children are somehow sub-human.

This chapter reviews leading trends in current research, policy and practice on children's rights, some common omissions, and what we could gain by renewed attention to the power at the centre of the Children in Charge series. The 1989 Convention on the Rights of the Child (UNCRC) (United Nations 1989), almost as old as JKP, has led to a child rights industry which, I suggest, partly shares the view of children as sub-human or not yet fully human and therefore needing their own set of rights that differ from adults' rights. Children's rights tend to be defined in ways that are equally well covered by concepts of needs, welfare and best interests, and which miss the power of rights. The 3Ps are useful when analysing the 54 UNCRC Articles but, as I will review, each P can be used to distort understanding of the related rights.

To begin with protection rights, these are often cited to help children to 'feel safe'. Yet feeling safe is not a right because rights are not about feelings, since these cannot be willed or enforced. No one can be forced to feel safe or can will (control) their own or others' feelings about fear or safety. And feelings are relative; some people will feel calm about matters that terrify other people. No one therefore has an actual right to feel safe. Rights are partly legal statements that, in theory at least, can be enforced in the courts, which examine behaviours, not feelings, since behaviours can be observed, reported and controlled. Rights aim to protect children from real dangers, from neglect, abuse and discrimination.

Undue stress on children 'feeling safe' risks trivialising rights when attention concentrates on nurseries, homes, schools and other fairly safe contexts. Paradoxically, protection rights can be used to set rigorous but petty standards that control adults and children, restrict their freedoms, punish adventurousness, and divert attention from children's experiences when protection is seriously needed: against exploitation, torture, cruel and inhuman or degrading treatment, illicit transfer abroad, abduction and trafficking, hazardous labour, illicit drugs, arbitrary arrest or detention, recruitment into armed conflict and violations of privacy.

The UNCRC is sometimes criticised for overemphasising children's vulnerable need for protection. But this forgets that modern human rights began from philosophers' desire to protect autonomous 'Man' from interference so that he could be self-determining, free to think and act and preserve his privacy as he chose, so long as this did not harm anyone else. The international human rights treaties agreed in the late 1940s were developed from the Nuremberg Nazi trials, primarily in order to protect everyone from the atrocities and suffering inflicted by the Nazis in the Second World War. Critics who claim that the UNCRC is too 'Western' overlook how its standards are vital for every child in the world, especially in the poorest countries. Children's right to protection from armed conflict is violated every day by bombing of urban areas, schools and hospitals. Perhaps there is a covert adult-centrism when researchers prefer to look at adults who are kindly working in safe 'child-centred' arenas, instead of examining the many areas where millions of children and adults suffer terribly from the dangers of (adults') military and economic policies?

With the next P, provision rights, researchers similarly tend to concentrate on children using fairly well-resourced services and centres. Yet the UN Conventions (such as in 1948 and 1966 as well as in 1989) also concern provision for the billions of deprived people of all ages in the world. There are provision rights to basic necessities that support wellbeing: healthcare, education, an adequate standard of living, free services run by competent staff, support for families, resources to respect everyone's economic, social and cultural rights, informative and respectful mass media, asylum, and services to aid recovery and reintegration after abuse and emigration.

The third P, participation rights, linked to freedom and self-determination, might be respected as the most adult-like set of rights, but it is too often reduced into Article 12, 'The child's right to express views freely in all matters affecting the child', with less attention to whether children are actually heard or their views are acted on seriously. Children may be presented with quasi-shopping lists, and asked what more resources and opportunities they would like to enjoy. Again the range, seriousness and power of these rights are too easily lost. These include rights to life and survival, a name, identity and nationality, contact with the child's own family or the best alternative, and respect for the child's cultural background, worth and inherent human dignity. There are vital freedoms of expression and information, of thought, conscience and religion, of association and peaceful assembly, besides all-age rights to rest, leisure and recreation, and to participate freely in cultural life and the arts. Crucial rights include due legal process that prevents wrongful punishments and imprisonment.

Rights are claims against injustice, remedies for wrongs, and international legal structures that hold governments and their agencies to account, as UNCRC Articles 42–54 enshrine. This is denied by the current fad for helping children to write their own wish-lists of rights, empty of political power. Instead, while in the UK, the US and many other countries' governments are deriding human rights, we should be helping everyone to understand, respect and exercise their rights, as the UNCRC says, 'in the spirit of peace, dignity, tolerance, freedom, equality and solidarity'. Mary John's Children in Charge series on rights and power supports this endeavour.

References

Alderson, P. (2008) *Young Children's Rights: Exploring Beliefs, Principles and Practice* (Children in Charge), second edition. London: Jessica Kingsley Publishers.

Griffith, R. (1998) *Educational Citizenship and Independent Learning* (Children in Charge). London: Jessica Kingsley Publishers.

John, M. (2003) *Children's Rights and Power: Charging up for a New Century* (Children in Charge). London: Jessica Kingsley Publishers.

Kiddle, C. (1999) *Traveller Children: A Voice for Themselves* (Children in Charge). London: Jessica Kingsley Publishers.

United Nations (1989) *Convention on the Rights of the Child.* Geneva: Office of the High Commissioner. www.ohchr.org/EN/ProfessionalInterest/Pages/CRC.aspx (accessed 7 July 2017).

* * *

PRISCILLA ALDERSON is Professor Emerita of Childhood Studies, University College London Institute of Education. Books include *The Politics of Childhoods Real and Imagined: Practical Application of Critical Realism and Childhood Studies*, Vol. 2 (Routledge, 2016), *Childhoods Real and Imagined: An Introduction to Critical Realism and Childhood Studies*, Vol. 1 (Routledge, 2013), and *The Ethics of Research with Children and Young People: A Practical Handbook*, with Virginia Morrow (Sage, revised third edition, 2011). More details at http://iris.ucl.ac.uk/iris/browse/profile?upi=DPALD60

13

Educational Psychology

The Past 30 Years

BARBARA KELLY

Educational psychology in the UK remains a small profession but one that is particularly distinctive in engaging in an ongoing challenge to radically reform its role and impact. Educational psychology has existed since the early twentieth century. Initially, the professional focus was narrow and much of the work was in assessing children's eligibility for alternative education in special schools (Gillham 1999). Traditionally, educational psychologists assessed individual children using psychometric tests and other assessments, the very use of which could be seen to endorse the view that observed deficits of learning, behaviour and emotional adjustment were exclusively within the child (Blythe and Miller 1996). The child deficit model was reflected in legislation describing and categorising children's needs as late as the 1950s, for example in the Maladjusted Special Educational Treatment (Scotland) Regulations (1954) and the Report of the Committee on Maladjusted Children (The Underwood Report 1955).

Today the situation is very different and the educational psychologist has an emancipated role, operating more clearly in line with evidence about factors and interventions most likely to promote educational success and wellbeing. The central challenge for educational psychology has been to respond directly to the range of emotional, social, economic and political forces shaping the individual development and destiny of children and young people, abandoning the narrow child-deficit-focused role of the past. Today's educational psychologists consult with schools and work with parents and organisations to support them to create positive experiences for children and young people. This wider and more complex identity has, at many points, anticipated contemporary evidence and vision for promoting effective education and the wellbeing of children and young people.

In the past 30 years, educational psychology has sought to establish key definitions, contexts and processes underlying positive change and how this might be realised for individuals, families, schools and other organisations involved in the development and education of children and young people. The major focus has been to clarify and construct a role relevant to emerging evidence on what approaches are most effective in achieving this.

Educational psychology's radical reworking of its role began in earnest in the 1970s with professionals reflecting on and expressing dissatisfaction about their prescriptive role in child assessment. Their role had essentially become moribund in the face of increasing insight and evidence from diverse sources (including education, psychology, sociology and human welfare and rights) which looked to the values, beliefs and contexts that promote or hinder child development and wellbeing. These disciplines increasingly highlighted the power and influence of context on individual outcomes. Research found schools to be complex organisations whose impact on children was far from straightforward and sometimes linked to the child's development of emotional, behavioural and learning difficulties. A far-reaching shift in perspective began within educational psychology, creating a complex process of evolution, moving professional values and practice away from a limited child deficit model and more towards a social processes model – that is, towards a fuller understanding of what experiences affect children and young people for good or ill.

The considerable complexity and challenge presented by this shift influenced professional debate, often reflecting anxiety within the profession about the opposition and lack of understanding it might attract from schools, parents and others. The idea that the ethos and ecology of a school has powerful influences on a child's potential to learn and develop was radical. It carried with it the implication that the school bears some responsibility for child outcomes and that the educational psychologist's role should necessarily become more discerning, advising on how to create a more effective school rather than solely focusing on the deficits identified by schools as being 'within the child'. Worries about the dissonance created for clients of educational psychology, which now challenged longstanding values and perceptions about schools, consumed many journal articles and conference debates in the 1980s and 1990s, resulting in an impasse and to some extent in the temporary loss of professional confidence and direction (Stobie 2002).

A key factor in helping to shape a meaningful identity and values for the profession has been the slow but steady appearance and acceptance of both values and evidence strongly supporting the direction and aims of contemporary educational psychology away from the inequity of child-deficit-focused practice. A major proponent in this shift in perspective was psychologist Bill Gillham, whose edited volume *Reconstructing Educational Psychology* (1978) summarised the concerns, beliefs and aspirations of a new generation of 'constructionist' practitioners. Gillham's position as a social constructionist psychologist was supported by developmental psychologist Urie Bronfenbrenner who in 1979 published his influential *Ecology of Human Development.*

In essence the constructionist perspective incorporated the ideas and the increasing evidence that society, organisations and individuals create, act on and negotiate interpretations of what is 'real'. Constructionist practitioners stated that this process of creating shared reality can be central in generating and fostering both inequality and equality. From a constructionist perspective, an exclusive focus on a child's presenting difficulties – the 'deficit model' – excludes a full understanding of the social and educational context. A consequence of the deficit model is that the need to change is located within the child, while the responsibility and potential for change in key social contexts is overlooked. Following a deficit model, educational psychologists would be working in isolation, and by not educating schools, families and communities about the impact of their involvement and potential to influence outcomes for children and young people, they effectively collude in reducing potential for growth and development.

Profoundly relevant illustrations of this were provided by the work of the first professor of child psychiatry in the United Kingdom, Michael Rutter. He, along with many others throughout the 1970s and 1980s, created an immense knowledge and evidence base about the relative impact and effectiveness of individual schools. This was done by undertaking research which compared schools of similar size, taking children from similar social backgrounds and similar levels of social disadvantage. Despite their similarities, these schools were found to differ radically in their actions and (it was hypothesised) in the later outcomes for young people. A key question was whether any school can actively help its students to overcome the adverse effects of economic disadvantage and family adversity.

In their book *Fifteen Thousand Hours: Secondary Schools and Their Effects on Children* (Rutter *et al.* 1982), Rutter and his colleagues showed that schools can indeed make a difference to young people. In a three-year study of a dozen secondary schools in a large urban area, Rutter's team found that some schools were demonstrably better than others at promoting the academic and social success of their students. There were clear and interesting differences between schools that promoted success and those that appeared to fail to do so, providing important clues to the kind of educational reform that might allow inner-city schools to act to provide a positive and protective influence on students: students who, for a dozen years during their formative period of development, would have spent as many of their waking hours at school as at home – some 15,000 hours in all.

Inevitably, aspects of this work were challenged, but the importance of this major area of research for educational psychology was in its demonstration that there are identifiable ways in which organisational behaviours differ and which may promote or diminish the wellbeing of individuals. This work continues in the ongoing development of a school effectiveness evidence base, and in groundbreaking work demonstrating the nature of social and interpersonal processes underpinning school effectiveness (Kratochwill 2014; Leana 2011).

As detailed above, the major shift in the values, beliefs and practices within educational psychology over the past 30 years was prompted by emerging ideas about the influence of contexts and systems and the impact they can have on the behaviour, beliefs, aspirations, wellbeing and achievement of those within them – staff as well as pupils. In adopting a very much wider model of professional practice, educational psychology now has to address a wide range of areas in systematic and increasingly evidence-based ways. Assessment and intervention related to key aspects of school ethos require skilled consultation, research skills and the provision of effective interpersonal support to enable improvement and development. There is no doubt that supporting change for individuals and for organisations is very challenging, but a considerable amount of what might be termed 'concept to process' literature and related research and evidence has emerged in the past 10 to 15 years. This literature explores what processes need to be altered or established to promote effective interventions and outcomes. Much of the evidence underpinning the educational psychologist's current activities has emerged from the development of systematic frameworks for practice and the growing implementation science evidence base on how to promote effective change.

Kelly *et al.* (2008) provided the concept of 'complementary frameworks for practice' which helped to differentiate, describe and clarify key concepts and types of work related to now very diverse practice areas. Key among these frameworks is the executive problem-solving framework (Monsen and Frederickson 2008, 2016) which reflected yet another shift in perspective from simple constructionism to critical realism, creating a combined model which takes into account different types of evidence about social processes and related factors when addressing issues and problems from the individual to the organisational. This framework searches for different types of evidence about a problem and collates this to ensure that all angles and issues are captured. The role of the educational psychologist applying this framework is to focus on factors or experiences affecting the child, school, family and community which may play a part in causing or maintaining problems. For example, a school may refer a child for serious non-attendance. To establish why this is happening requires exploration of a range of hypotheses about the child and their circumstances and feelings as well as the response adopted by the school and parents to promote good school attendance. Family circumstances are likely to contribute to attendance at school, as are aspects of communities. In any particular case of non-attendance the educational psychologist explores the unique combination of factors involved and draws on research evidence to provide detailed steps and interventions to enable attendance to improve. The understanding that frameworks for practice have different uses and levels of influence has allowed a range of concept- and practice-specific frameworks to be developed, making the complexity of the educational psychologist's tasks more focused and manageable (Kelly and Perkins 2012; Kelly, Woolfson and Boyle 2016).

Greater understanding and evidence on what drives change and improvement have been provided by 'implementation science', a discipline that has arisen in response to a global failure to replicate controlled interventions predictably and successfully in real-world contexts. Implementation science has relevance across a range of change-related professions, for example medicine and health. It has provided evidence and substantiated key concepts and processes involved in creating successful change in schools. A powerful review of this work and its implications in educational contexts has emerged recently with a key focus for psychology in education in Kelly and Perkins' *Handbook of Implementation Science for Psychology in Education* (2012). This book explores the evidence and processes supporting effective change and is an endorsement of the need for a specialised but wide professional focus such as that identified and developed by educational psychology over the past 30 years.

The discipline of educational psychology anticipated and understood the need for its role to be both specialised and wide-ranging. At this point it would be difficult to suggest that it should be otherwise given the substantial evidence accruing about the complex nature of the task of improving outcomes for children and young people. In the next three decades an exploration of the nature and role of evidence may need to become central to understanding and demonstrating the processes, impact and outcomes of educational psychology. In its 'real world' professional context, as opposed to controlled experimental contexts, educational psychology will be required to develop a more sophisticated understanding and application of evidence-related frameworks. The 'Typology of Evidence' proposed by Boyle and Kelly (2016) is designed to drive a clearer approach to measures of effectiveness in live as opposed to highly controlled contexts.

Policy development and implementation require the type of real-world frameworks evinced by educational psychology and implementation science, and the expertise developing in educational psychology about the many levels of work required to create effective implementation should guarantee that their involvement in improving experiences and outcomes for children is more widely understood and appreciated to be cutting edge.

References

Blythe, E. and Miller, J. (eds) (1996) *Exclusion from School: Inter-Professional Issues for Policy and Practice*. London: Routledge.

Boyle, J. and Kelly, B. (2016) 'The Role of Evidence in Educational Psychology.' In B. Kelly, L. Woolfson and J. Boyle (eds) *Frameworks for Practice in Educational Psychology: A Textbook for Trainees and Practitioners*, second edition. London: Jessica Kingsley Publishers.

Bronfenbrenner, U. (1979) *The Ecology of Human Development: Experiments by Nature and Design*. Cambridge, MA: President and Fellows of Harvard College.

Gillham, B. (ed.) (1978) *Reconstructing Educational Psychology*. London: Croom Helm.

Gillham, B. (1999) 'The writing of *Reconstructing Educational Psychology*.' *Educational Psychology in Practice 14*, 4, 220–221.

Kelly, B. and Perkins, D. (2012) *Handbook of Implementation Science for Psychology in Education*. New York: Cambridge University Press.

Kelly, B., Woolfson, L. and Boyle, J. (eds) (2008) *Frameworks for Practice in Educational Psychology: A Textbook for Trainees and Practitioners*, first edition. London: Jessica Kingsley Publishers.

Kelly, B., Woolfson, L. and Boyle, J. (eds) (2016) *Frameworks for Practice in Educational Psychology: A Textbook for Trainees and Practitioners*, second edition. London: Jessica Kingsley Publishers.

Kratochwill, T. R. (2014) 'School-Based Problem Solving Consultation: Plotting a New Course for Evidence-Based Research and Practice in Consultation.' In W. P. Erchul and S. M. Sheridan (eds) *Handbook of Research in School Consultation*, second edition. New York: Routledge.

Leana, C. (2011) 'The missing link in school reform.' *Stanford Social Innovation Review 9*, 4, 30–35.

Monsen, J. and Frederickson, N. (2008) 'The Monsen *et al.* Problem-Solving Model Ten Years On.' In B. Kelly, L. Woolfson and J. Boyle (eds) *Frameworks for Practice in Educational Psychology: A Textbook for Trainees and Practitioners*, first edition. London: Jessica Kingsley Publishers.

Monsen, J. and Frederickson, N. (2016) 'The Monsen Problem-Solving Model – Problem Analysis as a Guide to Decision Making, Problem Solving and Action within Applied Psychological Practice.' In B. Kelly, L. Woolfson and J. Boyle (eds) *Frameworks for Practice in Educational Psychology: A Textbook for Trainees and Practitioners*, second edition. London: Jessica Kingsley Publishers.

Rutter, M., Maughan, B., Mortimore, P. and Ouston, P., with Smith, A. (1982) *Fifteen Thousand Hours: Secondary Schools and Their Effects on Children.* Cambridge, MA: Harvard University Press.

Stobie, I. (2002) 'Processes of change and continuity: Part 1.' *Educational Psychology in Practice 18*, 3, 203–212.

The Underwood Report (1955) *Report of the Committee on Maladjusted Children.* London: HMSO.

* * *

BARBARA KELLY is Director of the MSc in Educational Psychology, School of Psychological Sciences and Health, University of Strathclyde. Her current areas of interest include implementation science and developing evidence-based practice frameworks for teaching and practice in educational psychology. Recent publications include *Frameworks for Practice in Educational Psychology: A Textbook for Trainees and Practitioners*, second edition (Jessica Kingsley Publishers, 2016), *Handbook of Implementation Science for Psychology in Education* (Cambridge University Press, 2012), 'Parents and the preschool PATHS (Promoting Alternative Thinking Strategies) curriculum' (*Journal of Children's Services*, 2015) and 'Implementing implementation science: Reviewing the quest to develop methods and frameworks for effective implementation' (*Journal of Neurology and Psychology*, 2013).

14

Social Work

JOYCE LISHMAN

As I briefly reflect over the past 30 years in social work, it strikes me that an overarching theme has been 'change and continuity'. The elements of this continuity are:

- the values and ethics base of social work

- social work as an activity which has to span, in understanding and intervention, both the individual and the structural world

- a person-centred and relationship-based approach to working

- a recognition of the importance of research and evidence in developing policy and practice.

What have been the major elements of change?

Social work is a professional activity which has always been regulated by law and social policy, with consequent changes. It has also therefore had to respond to changes in ideology, from the Keynesian–Beveridge welfare principles of freedom from want, squalor and poverty (which led to the introduction of the NHS and National Insurance, when we really believed we were in it together) to the current principle of austerity and consequent severe cuts in welfare.

More positively, the values underpinning social work have become much more ethnically diverse and tolerant of different ways of managing race, disability and gender. Old age, however, tends to continue to be viewed as problematic – a drain on resources.

Over the past 30 years, external changes and challenges arose in major ways. The first was the political context and change in ideology from Beveridge's principles to austerity. For a detailed example of the impact of this change, I'd recommend watching Ken Loach's film *I, Daniel Blake*, which communicates the reality of this shift more vividly than I can.

The second (writing from a Scottish perspective) has been devolution in Scotland. This has led to major changes in relation to the integration of social policy and social work practice across the UK. In Scotland, social work continues to include work with both children and adults. In Northern Ireland health and social care are more integrated and that is currently Scotland's ambition. The division in England between child and family social work, and social work with older people, is exemplified by two conflicting reports on social work education carried out by Martin Narey (2014) and David Croisdale-Appleby (2014) respectively. The former placed a focus on developing practitioners to do 'child protection', while the latter had a particular focus on adult work and the importance of working across the life course, and this tension has yet to be resolved.

Prior to these reports, Eileen Munro's (2011) report on child care and child protection had revealed the problematic issue in child care of reporting and paperwork. Findings included the compliance with rules and regulations at the expense of professional judgement drawn from building a professional relationship with the child and family.

Future challenges for social work

Internally for social work, its challenges arise from one of its strengths: its breadth. How do we maintain the integration between child care, adult care and mental health and, in Scotland, criminal justice?

I see the growing promotion of integration of health and social work as really positive, but there are still big question marks over how this is happening in practice, as the transfer of money from acute services to more general care services has not been happening in the way that it needs to. In addition, the integration of health and social care is a major challenge due to the danger that social work becomes 'lost' in the health service.

Social work is a critically valuable profession which has a nuanced individual–structural understanding of the challenges faced by people who may be clients or service users, and employs complex forms of intervention. It is important that in the future we do not allow the importance of social work to be overlooked or neglected.

References

Croisdale-Appleby, D. (2014) *Re-visioning Social Work Edication: An Independent Review*. London: Department of Health.

Munro, E. (2011) *The Munro Review of Child Protection: Final Report*. London: Department for Education.

Narey, M. (2014) *Making the Education of Social Workers Consistently Effective*. London: Department for Education.

* * *

JOYCE LISHMAN has worked with children and families. She became Head of the School of Applied Social Studies and is now Emeritus Professor at the Robert Gordon University. Among other publications, she edited the *Handbook for Practice Learning in Social Work and Social Care*, third edition (Jessica Kingsley Publishers, 2015).

15

Changing Views on Safeguarding Children Since 1987

HARRIET WARD

Jessica Kingsley Publishers was founded in 1987. That year was also significant to me, personally, for it was the year that I returned to work following what would now be regarded as a very extended maternity leave. In 1987 I had three small sons, and the youngest was about to start school. I now have three small grandchildren, and the eldest is about to start school. So JKP has been publishing 'books that make a difference' for a generation; and during those 30 years I have been learning about parenting and its implications for early childhood development both as an academic researcher and also, hands on, as a parent and grandparent myself.

Before my maternity leave I had been a social worker, but during my leave I began studying for a PhD on the relationship between the public responsibilities of the state and the private responsibilities of parents when children were deemed to be in need of protection in the late nineteenth century. This was the beginning of a lifelong addiction to research, and I never returned to practice. Instead I embarked on a new career as an academic, undertaking a programme of empirical research into child welfare interventions and their outcomes, mostly commissioned to inform national policy and practice. During much of that time I have been privileged to work closely with various editors at JKP, who have published almost all of the most significant studies undertaken by myself and the research centre that I directed at Loughborough University.

In 1987 I was appointed as Academic Secretary to the Department of Health Independent Working Party on Child Care Outcomes. Our role was to work out a means of assessing whether and in what ways placing children in care made a difference to their life chances. The deliberations of the working party provide a useful starting point for exploring how our understanding of child protection has changed over the past 30 years, for while there are many similarities, there have also been a number of significant changes, which reflect not only how the knowledge base has grown, but also how the public discourse and the political and policy contexts have changed.

First, and it seems unbelievable now, the words 'abuse' and 'neglect' were barely mentioned over the three years that the working party sat and, indeed, we had to be reminded to include questions on these issues in the first draft of the assessment materials (the Looking After Children programme) that were later implemented nationally. I had qualified as a social worker in 1973, at the very end of a 'golden' age that had lasted since the end of the First World War, during which time the maltreatment of children, an issue of great concern to the Victorians, had either ceased to exist or, more likely, ceased to be part of the public consciousness as other, more pressing issues had intervened. Physical abuse was rediscovered in the

1960s, with Kempe's seminal work on the 'battered baby syndrome' (Kempe *et al.* 1962); sexual abuse reappeared as an issue in the 1980s, the complex web of reactions which it engenders epitomised by the Cleveland inquiry into the removal of 121 children from parents who might – or might not – have been sexually abusing them (Butler-Sloss 1988). Neglect and emotional abuse were not regarded as significant issues until this century, when their potentially long-term consequences in terms of children's social, emotional and cognitive development came into sharper focus as new strands of research began to identify how such maltreatment in the early years impacts across key areas of growth, including children's neurobiological development, and how these, among other adverse childhood experiences, can have long-term consequences for both physical and mental health in adulthood (see Brown and Ward 2013 for a summary; also Felitti *et al.* 1998).

Second, the independent working party was holding its discussions while the Children Act 1989 was being debated in Parliament, and published its report in 1991 (Parker *et al.* 1991), the year the Act was implemented. This seminal Act set the rationale for providing services within a child development framework. Whereas previous legislation had specified the circumstances under which parents might be regarded as 'unfit' and their children removed, the 1989 Act introduced a new concept of 'children in need' whom local authorities had a duty to support. A child might be taken to be 'in need' if:

(a) he is unlikely to achieve or maintain, or to have the opportunity of achieving or maintaining, a reasonable standard of health or development without the provision for him of services by a local authority...;

(b) his health or development is likely to be significantly impaired, or further impaired, without the provision for him of such services; or

(c) he is disabled.

Children Act 1989, Section 17.10

This conceptual shift was hugely significant, for it meant that the focus of enquiry could move from assessing risk to identifying need. Child maltreatment could be seen as one end of a spectrum of parental behaviours, rather than as an aberrant pattern that is entirely alien to the vast majority of the population. Child protection services could then be set within a range of provision both for children in need and parents, designed to strengthen families and, where necessary, help parents to overcome the adversities that led to maltreatment. Following the introduction of the Children Act 1989, a wide range of family support services was developed, and for many years the number of children in care was reduced.

Moreover, enabling children to achieve or maintain 'a reasonable standard of health or development' could be articulated as an uncontroversial objective for all professionals with responsibilities for children, from those providing universal services, such as education, to those offering more specialist provision for children with high levels of need. 'It takes a whole village to raise a child': setting services within a child development framework provided an incentive to develop more integrated services in which professionals could work more closely together towards the same objectives. Fifteen years after the Children Act 1989, the Children Act 2004 provided the legislative basis for extended reorganisation of services aimed at greater integration.

Finally, in order to develop their methodology for assessing the outcomes of care, it had been necessary for the members of the independent working party to reach a consensus concerning the purpose of placing children away from home. Should the care system focus on meeting children's material needs – providing food, shelter and clothing – until they reached adulthood, or should it aspire to help children overcome the consequences of early adversities and meet their full potential? In the 1980s, the old Poor Law principle of 'less eligibility', that it was unethical for the state to provide a higher standard of care than the poorest 'independent labourer' was able to offer his or her family, still informed discourses about welfare, and it was acceptable to argue that care should not be aspirational. The working party's conclusion, that the ultimate purpose of the care system was to enable children who could not live with their birth families to 'achieve long-term wellbeing in adulthood', by offering consistently high standards of parenting designed to meet children's needs and help them overcome the consequences of abuse (Parker *et al.* 1991, p.105), was considered to be innovative at the time. However, it fitted in with the child development framework introduced by the Children Act 1989, which made it possible for care to be viewed not as a means of removing children from parents who were unfit so much as one element in a range of services designed to protect children from harm and enable them to reach their full potential.

Since the 1980s, there has been increasing awareness of the consequences of abuse and neglect; this has led to greater attention being paid to the educational, health and mental health needs of children who come into care, together with an acknowledgement that care leavers need better support as they move towards independence.

Initiatives such as Care Matters (Department for Education and Skills 2006) and Staying Put (Department for Education, Department for Work and Pensions and HM Revenue and Customs 2013) were introduced in order to help local authorities address these needs.

Conclusion

Of course reality has always fallen short of aspiration. Over the past 30 years we may have come a long way in acknowledging and understanding both the causes and the consequences of abuse and neglect, and in conceptualising how services might be better designed to meet the needs of children and families. There is also some evidence that, despite all the negative publicity, the majority of children who are looked after by local authorities achieve positive outcomes (see Ward, Brown and Hyde-Dryden 2014 for a summary). Studies in the Safeguarding Children Research Initiative, published by Jessica Kingsley Publishers, found that abused and neglected children who remained in care tended to do better in terms of both stability and outcomes than those who returned to birth families (Davies and Ward 2012; Farmer and Lutman 2012; Wade *et al.* 2011). Nevertheless, there are numerous problems across the whole spectrum of identification and responses to the needs of abused and neglected children that have never been addressed. To name but a few: tensions between agencies remain, and often result in delays in identifying and acting upon evidence of abuse and neglect; support to parents is often offered too late, and for too short a period; we know too little about which interventions are effective; and children who enter care often experience numerous changes of placement and insufficient understanding of their needs

(Davies and Ward 2012). It is only by taking a long view that we can see what progress has been made.

Finally, there are also concerns that progress that was made in the first two decades since Jessica Kingsley Publishers was founded may be jeopardised by changes introduced over the past ten years or so. A shift in ideology towards the vilification of families dependent on welfare has legitimised substantial cuts in benefits, thereby magnifying the challenges of parenting for many who are struggling, and making abuse and neglect more likely. The introduction of austerity measures following the financial crash of 2007–2008 has meant the loss of many family support services that were designed to prevent the occurrence of maltreatment and to ensure that children could safely remain with birth parents. In my view the greatest achievements in the field of child protection over the past 30 years have been the abandonment of the old Poor Law principle of 'less eligibility' and the shift towards developing a service based on meeting children's needs. It is important to fight to ensure that these endure.

References

Brown, R. and Ward, H. (2013) *Decision-Making within a Child's Timeframe: An Overview of Research Evidence for Family Justice Professionals Concerning Child Development and the Impact of Maltreatment* (Working Paper 16). Childhood Wellbeing Research Centre Report to the Department for Education. www.gov.uk/government/uploads/system/uploads/attachment_data/file/200471/Decision-making_within_a_child_s_timeframe.pdf (accessed 27 July 2017).

Butler-Sloss, E. (1988) *Report of the Inquiry into Child Abuse in Cleveland 1987* (Cm 412). London: HMSO.

Davies, C. and Ward, H. (2012) *Safeguarding Children Across Services: Messages from Research.* London: Jessica Kingsley Publishers.

Department for Education, Department for Work and Pensions and HM Revenue and Customs (2013) *Staying Put: Arrangements for Care Leavers Aged 18 Years and Above.* London: Department for Education.

Department for Education and Skills (2006) *Care Matters: Transforming the Lives of Children and Young People in Care*, Cm 6932. London: Department for Education and Skills.

Farmer, E. and Lutman, E. (2012) *Effective Working with Neglected Children and Their Families: Linking Interventions to Long-Term Outcomes*. London: Jessica Kingsley Publishers.

Felitti, V. J., Anda, R. F., Nordenberg, D., Williamson, D. F., Spitz, A. M. and Edwards, V. (1998) 'Relationship of childhood abuse and household dysfunction to many of the leading causes of death in adults: The Adverse Childhood Experiences (ACE) study.' *American Journal of Preventive Medicine 14*, 4, 245–258.

Kempe, C. H., Silverman, F. N., Steele, B. F., Droegemuller, W. and Silver, H. K. (1962) 'The battered child syndrome.' *Journal of the American Medical Association 181*, 17–24.

Parker, R., Ward, H., Jackson, S., Aldgate, J. and Wedge, P. (eds) (1991) *Looking After Children: Assessing Outcomes in Child Care*. London: HMSO.

Wade, J., Biehal, N., Farrelly, N. and Sinclair, I. (2011) *Caring for Abused and Neglected Children: Making the Right Decisions for Reunification or Long-Term Care*. London: Jessica Kingsley Publishers.

Ward, H., Brown, R. and Hyde-Dryden, G. (2014) *Assessing Parental Capacity to Change when Children are on the Edge of Care: An Overview of Research Evidence*. Loughborough University Centre for Child and Family Research for the Department of Education. https://dspace.lboro.ac.uk/dspace-jspui/bitstream/2134/18183/1/RR369_Assessing_parental_capacity_to_change_Final.pdf (accessed 27 July 2017).

* * *

HARRIET WARD is Research Professor at Loughborough University. She founded Loughborough's Centre for Child and Family Research (CCFR) in 2002 and directed it until she stepped down in April 2014. Between 2010 and 2015 she was also co-director of the government-funded Childhood Wellbeing Research Centre, a partnership between the Institute of Education, University of London, Loughborough University and the Personal Social Services Research Unit (PSSRU), University of Kent. She has over 30 years of experience both as a research director and field researcher, as an adviser to policy makers and service providers, and as a social work practitioner. She was awarded a CBE for services to children and families in June 2012. She has edited the Child Welfare Outcomes book series, published by Jessica Kingsley Publishers, since 2003.

Recent publications with Jessica Kingsley Publishers include *Costs and Consequences of Placing Children in Care* (with Lisa Holmes and Jean Soper; 2008), *Safeguarding Children Across Services: Messages from Research* (with Carolyn Davies; 2012) and *Safeguarding Babies and Very Young Children from Abuse and Neglect* (with Rebecca Brown and David Westlake; 2012).

16

30 Years of Social Work and the Media

MARTIN BARROW

When did it all go wrong between social workers and the media? You can do worse than to look back to 1987, exactly 30 years ago, to the Cleveland child abuse scandal. This was a profoundly disturbing case in which dozens of children were removed from their families on the basis of diagnoses given by two paediatricians. In the face of a public outcry the doctors were challenged and, eventually, many of the children were allowed to return home. By then, an entire community was traumatised and social workers, as well as paediatricians, had become demonised.

Cleveland was far from being the first case of its kind in which the competence of professionals tasked with child protection was questioned. But it came at a particularly sensitive moment, when the whole ethos of public service was being challenged by Margaret Thatcher's government (her 'There's no such thing as society' comment was also made in 1987; Margaret Thatcher Foundation 2017). The case remained in the public consciousness well beyond

Cleveland for several years, with a report by Elizabeth Butler-Sloss (1988) into the case, and implementation of the Children Act 1989. It weighed heavily on media coverage of cases that were investigated in the following years, such as the 'satanic abuse case' in Rochdale in 1990 and the Orkney abuse scandal in 1991 (Waterhouse 2014).

Just as 24-hour rolling TV news was gaining traction, the public's appetite for details of these cases appeared insatiable and social workers became big news. There was no turning back, and with each harrowing case came a demand for individuals to blame and to hold to account. I was news editor of *The Times* from 2008 to 2012, a tumultuous period for social work that included the serious case review into the death of Baby P (Shoesmith 2016) (a case that triggered a surge in interventions); the kidnapping of Shannon Matthews (*Yorkshire Evening Post* 2008); the life-threatening assault on two children by two brothers aged 10 and 11 in Edlington, Doncaster (Walker and Wainwright 2010); and the death by neglect and starvation of seven-year-old Khyra Ishaq in Birmingham (BBC News Online 2010).

Throughout this period the narrative around social work was relentlessly negative. They were all complex cases in which multiple agencies and individuals shared responsibility for the tragic outcome, yet social workers, invariably, were left to shoulder the blame. Police, doctors, teachers or the courts were rarely singled out by the media in cases of severe neglect or abuse, even when there was clear evidence of culpability. This situation persists to this day. There is no more powerful example of this than Sharon Shoesmith, who was dismissed as Director of Children's Services at Haringey Council in the wake of the Baby P case (Shoesmith 2016).

Why is this? The reasons are complex and vary from case to case, but a number of general points can be made. Social workers still feel more inhibited than most other public services in responding to criticism, through fear of breaching client confidentiality. Often this concern is well founded, but I have no doubt that there is room for more openness and transparency.

Social workers also lack an authoritative, national voice, such as the British Medical Association (BMA) for doctors or the National Union of Teachers (NUT) for teachers. Those who speak on their behalf are often beholden to other stakeholders including politicians, lawyers and even insurers. The head of children's services or chief executive of a local authority is unlikely to provide the robust soundbites that will give the headlines that frontline social workers would like to see in the next day's papers. In effect, officials are giving responses hardly changed from 30 years ago to a media that has changed beyond recognition.

Harsh financial reality means that newsrooms have fewer journalists struggling to produce more content than ever before around the clock. On the whole, journalists are younger and less experienced now than they were (just as social workers are), and they answer to editors who demand stories to be told succinctly and unambiguously. The presumption is that readers will drift away after a couple of hundred words, and that they want stories about people, not processes. This demands a simple narrative that does not lend itself to unpicking the complexities of a case involving multiple agencies. It requires a victim and somebody to blame. It requires grief, and it requires somebody calling for justice. Anything beyond that is unlikely to survive the first cut.

News organisations rarely send journalists to cover anything other than the highest-profile court cases. Reporters are highly unlikely to attend inquests or family courts. All nuances are lost in the scramble to distil lengthy and complex serious case reviews to just two or three bullet points and soundbites. Few specialist correspondents have survived the newsroom cull, but even they are likely to be swept aside by crime or political reporters for the biggest stories of failings in social services. This means that coverage is in the hands of journalists who don't know, or simply don't care, how the system works.

It would be wrong to suggest that there ever was a golden age in which journalists and social workers saw themselves as kindred spirits. But there is no doubt that the gulf between the two sides is as wide as it ever has been. Some of this is down to the politics of austerity. We know that dwindling resources have a huge impact on the effectiveness of social services. Yet any attempt to invoke austerity as a factor when things go wrong invites opprobrium.

Digital media offers some respite. There is a proliferation of outlets for social workers to share their views and experience, from The Guardian Professional Network (a collection of community sites that bring professionals together to share experiences from their working lives) to Facebook and Twitter. They can reach policy makers and commissioners of services and, occasionally, these stories spill over into the mainstream media. The challenge is to escape from the echo chamber to challenge public perceptions of social work.

Are social work and the media a hopeless case in 2017 and the age of post-truth? It certainly feels like a long way back. But it matters, profoundly, because without public support there can be no meaningful, lasting change.

Individual social workers have a role to play in challenging the narrative by celebrating their successes as publicly and as widely as possible. They can exert pressure on managers to be less defensive and show pride in the achievements of social work. Much of what social workers do doesn't get talked about because, ironically, it is taken for granted. In the end, it is about open, confident and inclusive leadership to engage with the media on equal terms.

References

BBC News Online (2010, 27 July) 'Starved girl Khyra Ishaq's death "was preventable".' www.bbc.co.uk/news/uk-england-birmingham-10770907 (accessed 24 July 2017).

Butler-Sloss, E. (1988) *Report of the Inquiry into Child Abuse in Cleveland 1987* (Cm 412). London: HMSO.

Margaret Thatcher Foundation (2017) Interview for *Women's Own* ('no such thing as society'). www.margaretthatcher.org/document/106689 (accessed 24 July 2017).

Shoesmith, S. (2016) *Learning from Baby P: The Politics of Blame, Fear and Denial.* London: Jessica Kingsley Publishers.

Walker, P. and Wainwright, M. (2010) 'Edlington brothers jailed for torture of two boys.' *The Guardian*, 22 January. www.theguardian.com/uk/2010/jan/22/edlington-brothers-jailed-torture-boys (accessed 24 July 2017).

Waterhouse, R. T. (2014) 'Satanic Abuse, False Memories, Weird Beliefs and Moral Panics.' Unpublished doctoral thesis, City University London.

Yorkshire Evening Post (2008, 11 March) 'Search for Shannon: Biggest inquiry since Yorkshire Ripper.' www.yorkshireeveningpost.co.uk/news/search-for-shannon-biggest-inquiry-since-yorkshire-ripper-1-2174139 (accessed 24 July 2017).

* * *

MARTIN BARROW is a journalist and writer, who specialises in health and social care. He worked for *The Times* for almost 25 years, including four years as news editor and two years as health editor. He has been a foster carer for eight years, and is co-editor of *Welcome to Fostering* with Andy Elvin, published in 2017 by Jessica Kingsley Publishers.

17

30 Years in the Field of Adoption and Foster Care

KIM GOLDING

The year 1987 was life-changing for me. I was a relatively newly qualified clinical psychologist and was embarking on motherhood. The birth of my son was a long way removed from the world of adoption and fostering but, unbeknown to me at the time, this latter world was on the threshold of great change.

It would be another decade before I took on the responsibility alongside colleagues to develop a support service for carers of children living in and adopted from care, but this service would be shaped by changes that were already starting. The 30 years during which my son has grown into an adult, and Jessica Kingsley Publishers has become a leading publisher in literature focused on adoption and fostering, have coincided with a period of intense scrutiny, research and change within the world of fostering and adoption.

The year 1987 was a point in time when views and attitudes were changing. In the previous decade the impact of high-profile cases of child abuse and familial child homicide, such as the death of Maria Colwell in 1973 (see Committee of Inquiry into the Care and Supervision Provided in Relation to Maria Colwell 1974), combined with seminal research as featured in *Children Who Wait: A Study of Children Needing Substitute Families* (Rowe and Lambert 1973), confronted social service commissioners and service developers with the reality of child abuse and the poor outcome for these children who entered the care system. The need for a flexible care system that could meet the need for a stable family life was highlighted.

Alongside this, the use of adoption was undergoing a radical shift from primarily infant adoptions shrouded in shame and secrecy towards adoption as a solution to provide a legal and permanent family life for older children in care where successful transition back to birth family was not possible or successful. There was increasing debate about the rights and needs of parents versus children, and recognition that we needed a care and adoption system that was flexible and could provide a range of options for children not able to live with birth parents. This eventually led to the 1989 Children's Act in England and Wales, followed by acts in 1995 for Northern Ireland and for Scotland.

The year 1987, and the subsequent shift in legislation in the following years, also signalled a change in our understanding of child development and the impact of adversity. Three decades of development and research into attachment theory by John Bowlby and his followers were finally leading to the acceptance that children need an attachment to a parent.

Child abuse and neglect was now seen as having long-lasting impacts on health and development. Child and family welfare became a focus of social care practice, with an emphasis on finding least-intrusive options and establishing partnership working with parents. Residential care was declining and foster care increasing, while contact arrangements were formalised.

By the time I was involved in the development of support services for carers and parents of children in or adopted from care at the beginning of this century, the term 'looked after children' was the established descriptor and the 1989 Act had become embedded in practice. Whether this made parental or children's needs paramount is open to debate, but there was increasing recognition of the mental health needs of children in and adopted from care. There was, however, little inter-agency working between health, social care and education to meet these needs. Fragmentary services and a lack of investment in support services were leading to instability and a lack of permanence for the children. As we entered a new century, the 'naughties', there was a raft of concern, advice, guidance and legislation which would lead to change in the way we recognised looked after children's needs and how we set up services to meet these. This was the backdrop to the development of our service in Worcestershire, which was to become the Integrated Service for Looked After and Adopted Children (ISL).

A document entitled *Every Child Matters* (ECM; Department for Education and Skills 2003) alongside two pieces of legislation, the Adoption and Children Act 2002, and the Children Act of 2004, were instrumental in shaping services for children, including those looked after and adopted from care. ECM focused all services working with children and young people on five outcomes seen as most important for them to lead happy and healthy lives. These were to be healthy, to stay safe, to enjoy and achieve, to make a positive contribution and to achieve economic wellbeing.

There was growing recognition that children growing up in or adopted from care were not getting close to achieving any of these outcomes. We needed interventions that took into account their past traumatic experience and the impact it was having on their current experience. In addition, the Children Act of 2004 was emphasising the importance of inter-agency working to achieve good outcomes. This paved the way for many services, like ours, being set up to promote multi-agency planning and partnership working. The third guidance, in the form of the Adoption and Children Act 2002, helped to focus attention onto the support needs of families who were caring for these vulnerable children. Support for the parents and carers so that they could provide a safe and healing parenting environment for the children was viewed as integral for services focused on achieving different outcomes for looked after and adopted children.

Against this background of advice and guidance we developed a consultation service for those parenting the children, which included the network around the children and family. This had the explicit aims to promote inter-agency and partnership working, alongside providing support for the parents and carers (see Dent and Golding 2006; Golding 2004, 2010, 2014). We also developed group work programmes to provide additional support and help for those parenting the children (see Golding 2006, 2007; Golding and Picken 2004). We provided the parents and carers with a model informed by the principles of dyadic developmental psychotherapy (DDP), which would help them provide therapeutic parenting. The group format provided an additional level of support as group members discovered they were not alone in the challenges that they were facing.

The Every Child Matters policy initiative was one of providing stability of family life for the children, provided through a range of options including foster, residential and kinship care, alongside adoption. One size was not seen to fit all, and the assessment and analysis of children's needs was increasingly informed by multi-agency perspectives. It is easy to paint a rosy picture of these years, supported as I was to be innovative and creative, but there were some salutary lessons along the way. Victoria Climbié (Laming 2003), for example, was an important wake-up call for those of us concerned to promote good multi-agency working. However, this was a period of time when I believe innovation was allowed to flourish and social care, health and education were thinking together about how to embed this into services.

In parallel to changes in policy, I have been privileged to work with children and families involved in adoption and the care system over a period of time that has seen our knowledge and understanding of the impact of relational trauma on mental health and emotional wellbeing increase. This growth of knowledge has built upon what we knew about attachment theory 30 years ago to embrace new research relating to neurodevelopment. This growth in knowledge has coincided with an injection of money to develop support services dedicated to growing and developing support interventions, and a renewed focus on successful parenting of the children living in care or adopted from care. For example, the Adoption Support Fund has been established in increasing recognition that adoption is not a 'happy ever after' option for children, but a family journey that presents a range of challenges and requires support and intervention at key points along this journey.

And so we come to the last decade and sadly, as is often the case, a child's death. In 2009 the death of Peter Connolly (Baby P) prompted outrage at perceived failures of social services, health and the police to protect Peter, and in its aftermath blame and recrimination raged between the government, the range of services and agencies involved, and the public. Lord Laming was commissioned to write another report in an effort to address these concerns (Laming 2009). Laming acknowledged work that had been done towards safeguarding children, but also highlighted much that was still needed. Following Peter's death, and the recognition of what was still not working to protect children, looked after children numbers have risen. For example, in Worcestershire, where I established our service, numbers of looked after children which hovered around 500 at the time of our service development have risen to current levels of approaching 700. The fallout from the death of Baby P still resonates today (see Shoesmith 2016). I believe this coincided with a time when social work was becoming increasingly threatened, and perhaps served as a handy scapegoat – financial constraints on public services have been a big driver. I have lived through unprecedented cuts in public services, and seen the hard decisions about reduction in services that this has led to. ISL has so far survived this austerity, but it has been reduced, the education element being hardest hit.

Our awareness of child safety has rightfully increased, but not always helpfully, as it has been accompanied by the rise of an increasingly risk-averse culture. In my opinion the combination of this culture with limited resources has focused services too narrowly on the immediate management of children in crisis and has placed less focus on good-quality prevention and early intervention. Social work has increasingly become a profession focused on targets and procedures rather than relationships with the families they are working with. A reduction in multi-disciplinary working and an increasing practice of lone working and personal responsibility appear to be contributing to a climate where rates of burnout and exhaustion are high. Children in care have been hit hard, and their numbers still increase.

However, there are also some positive developments. There is renewed interest in children's mental health, coupled with recognition of the impact of life experiences on children. Children's needs are being identified, although services continue to struggle to meet these needs. There has also been a drive to achieve more adoptions, in quicker timescales, for children. More haste can mean less speed, and it is important that assessment of adoptive families takes into account the complexity of the children who are adopted. However, the recognition that these families need specialist support is welcomed. This has been highlighted by the Adoption Support Services Act of 2005 and the subsequent use of the Adoption Support Fund, which aims to improve assessment and access to appropriate interventions for adopted children and their families.

We are currently on the verge of major developments in social care services. For example, the development of regionalisation of adoption agencies is being considered to change the way adoption services are offered. Serious case review procedures are being overhauled as these are seen to raise the same concerns over and over again, but the recommendations are not leading to the needed change. We need to learn the lessons from child deaths in a way that is embedded in practice. It is too early to determine the threats or successes that these developments will bring, but I trust and hope that Jessica Kingsley Publishers will be around for another 30 years as we continue to learn, develop our knowledge, influence national policy and promote service development in a way that can truly meet the needs of this courageous and vulnerable population of children and young people looked after or adopted from care.

References

Committee of Inquiry into the Care and Supervision Provided in Relation to Maria Colwell (1974) *Report of the Committee of Inquiry into the Care and Supervision Provided by Local Authorities and Other Agencies in Relation to Maria Colwell and the Co-Ordination Between Them* (Chairman: T. G. Field-Fisher). London: HMSO.

Dent, H. R. and Golding, K. S. (2006) 'Engaging the Network: Consultation for Looked After and Adopted Children.' In K. S. Golding, H. R. Dent, R. Nissim and E. Stott (eds) *Thinking Psychologically About Children Who Are Looked After and Adopted: Space for Reflection*. Chichester: John Wiley & Sons Ltd.

Department for Education and Skills (2003) *Every Child Matters*. London: Department for Education and Skills.

Golding, K. S. (2004) 'Providing specialist psychological support to foster carers: A consultation model.' *Child and Adolescent Mental Health 9*, 2, 71–76.

Golding, K. S. (2006) 'Finding the Light at the End of the Tunnel: Parenting Interventions for Adoptive and Foster Carers.' In K. S. Golding, H. R. Dent, R. Nissim and E. Stott (eds) *Thinking Psychologically About Children Who Are Looked After and Adopted: Space for Reflection*. Chichester: John Wiley & Sons Ltd.

Golding, K. S. (2007) 'Developing group-based parent training for foster and adoptive parents.' *Adoption and Fostering 31*, 3, 39–48.

Golding, K. S. (2010) 'Multi-agency and specialist working to meet the mental health needs of children in care or adopted.' *Clinical Child Psychology and Psychiatry 15*, 4, 1–15.

Golding, K. S. (2014) 'Multi-Agency and Specialist Working to Meet the Mental Health Needs of Children in Care and Adopted.' In M. Tarren-Sweeney and A. Vetere (eds) *Mental Health Services for Vulnerable Children and Young People: Support for Children Who Are, or Have Been, in Foster Care*. Oxford: Routledge.

Golding, K. S. and Picken, W. (2004) 'Group work for foster carers caring for children with complex problems.' *Adoption and Fostering 28*, 1, 25–37.

Laming, W. (2003) *The Victoria Climbié Inquiry: Report of an Inquiry*. London: The Stationery Office.

Laming, W. (2009) *The Protection of Children in England: A Progress Report.* London: The Stationery Office.

Rowe, J. and Lambert, L. (1973) *Children Who Wait: A Study of Children Needing Substitute Families.* London: British Association for Adoption and Fostering.

Shoesmith, S. (2016) *Learning from Baby P: The Politics of Blame, Fear and Denial.* London: Jessica Kingsley Publishers.

* * *

KIM GOLDING, BSc, MSc, D. Clin. Psy. AFBPsS, is a clinical psychologist who worked with children and families within the NHS for 30 years. Kim has always been interested in parenting, and collaborating with parents or carers to develop their parenting skills tailored to the particular needs of the children they are caring for. She is a consultant and trainer in DDP, an intervention for children whose earliest experience has been traumatic. In 2015 Kim started working independently to provide training, consultation and supervision to a range of individuals and teams in the UK, Europe, Australia and New Zealand. Kim is the author of several books written for parents, educational staff and practitioners supporting children with experience of developmental trauma.

18

Other People's Children

Adoption

SALLY DONOVAN

Thirty years ago, when Jessica Kingsley Publishers was being formed, I was 18 and about to embark on my first experience of parenting. After finishing sixth-form college I took the Eurolines coach to Paris and started work as an au-pair for an Anglo-French couple – a floppy-haired British banker who had something of a blond Hugh Grant about him and a beautiful Parisian woman who spoke English like Princess Diana. I lived with them in their rented house just off Place Charles de Gaulle and cared for their one-year-old son Pascal. It was kind of normal back then to go to a foreign country, move in with people you knew virtually nothing about and, with no experience, look after their precious child.

By luck and a bit of judgement the arrangement worked well. They got live-in childcare and I got to be based in central Paris and have the time of my life.

There were a lot of foreign au-pairs in the city and among us we shared knowledge about casual babysitting jobs.

It was a way of making some 'no strings' extra money. Someone's 'Madame' (not that kind) would have a friend who had a child who needed watching for an afternoon. An address and instructions about how to get into the apartment building would be provided and there you would find yourself, in a stranger's apartment, looking after their wide-eyed child. This was (and may still be) common practice among the French upper class in the city.

One afternoon I babysat for an aristocratic family, the kind that grace the society pages of *Paris Match*. The only instruction I was given, before Madame swept out in a cloud of Chanel, was 'Do *not* let him damage the table.' I endured five very long hours of trying to divert their determined three-year-old from doing just that. Being who they were, the table was Louis XV and the little boy's weapon of choice was a metal racing car. I was not entirely successful at carrying out the one instruction I had been given. Back then I worried about the table. Now both blessed and burdened with a working knowledge of attachment, I think about that child. Perhaps it's no wonder he had a thing for his parents' heirlooms. He knew what was precious and how to get a reaction (attachment-seeking, not attention-seeking!).

Thirty years on and I parent through adoption children who belong, in a biological sense, to someone else and who have experience of being passed around. Who knows what 'attachment style' that little French boy with a grudge against Louis XV might have grown up with, but nevertheless he was clean, warm, well fed, demonstrably loved and, I'm guessing, safe. My children (I'll refer to them as 'my' children for grammatical prudence and not through any desire to stamp ownership) weren't born into a tastefully furnished life in the XVIth arrondissement. The details aren't mine to share, but in bullish moments I wonder why it could be that nobody went to jail (if the victims had been adults then someone surely would have). The impact upon them as individuals has been significant and will be lifelong. That's not to say they haven't healed and flourished in many ways, but the trauma resulting from the abuse they experienced is evident every single day.

The job of understanding that trauma and the behaviours rooted in it, and learning to parent appropriately, has been, and I suspect will be, my life's work (something my 18-year-old self would never have guessed). It is harder than I could ever have imagined and it has torn away many of my old beliefs and values: many that I had thought of as indisputable. The process of becoming the parent my children need me to be has been one of taking apart who I once was, and rebuilding myself from the bottom up. I've had to learn that they see the world differently to me, in fundamental ways: where I see plenty, they see danger of famine; where I see kindness, they see a motive; where I see support, they see loss of control. Not all the old parts of me have been discarded. Some hang on by their fingernails because they are part of my survival and core to who I am, and some have come in useful (ridiculous determination, never able to do things by half). It's a way of life that exposes us to our potential depths as well as our heights.

The lion's share of my parenting is done and, although we still fall over at times, the foundations are strong and I feel positive about the future. I've made mistakes, but I have done my best with the resources I've had, and there is little of substance I would do differently. I'm not keen on expressions of pride, but when taking the long view I occasionally get a sense, in a small domestic way, of how enormous our achievement has been. Plenty of furniture (none of it Louis XV) has got in the way, but we've aced some big wins: the biggest being permanence.

Permanence is the golden ticket in terms of building strong foundations for children's futures and, right now, the state and the judiciary are wrestling with its different forms and their relative benefits and drawbacks. There are some enormous tensions playing out that buckle and strain against each other like vast tectonic plates. Some of the language used about adoption ('draconian', 'forced', 'heart', 'forever'…) is indicative of that strain and will not, I fear, progress things in meaningful and thoughtful ways. Where this will take us over the next 30 years is hard to guess. Will adoption still exist as an option for permanence? I don't know, but I hope the baby doesn't get thrown out with the bath water (something I'm pleased to report that even as an 18-year-old au-pair I never did).

As Jessica Kingsley Publishers celebrates its thirtieth year, I witness my children starting to make their own way in the world. It is both wonderful and terrifying (will that darned cause-and-effect thinking *ever* fall into place?), and the 'drip drip' of worry is constant. Life will never be straightforward for us and I'm mostly (but sometimes not) at ease with that. My role and influence are diminishing and my life, which has been dominated by hard-core parenting, is starting to open up again. It's liberating and quite exciting. I might even get back to Paris, rediscover that plucky 18-year-old and tell her she did all right.

* * *

SALLY DONOVAN is an adoptive parent and author of the adoption memoir *No Matter What* (Jessica Kingsley Publishers, 2013), as well as *The Unofficial Guide to Adoptive Parenting* (Jessica Kingsley Publishers,

2014) and children's book *Billy Bramble and the Great Big Cook Off* (Jessica Kingsley Publishers, 2016). She is editor of *Adoption Today* and is a member of various government committees tasked with improving adoption support and mental health services.

19

Adult Safeguarding

MICHAEL MANDELSTAM

Introduction

Thirty years ago, I started writing for Jessica Kingsley Publishers on social care and the law. Since then, we have published many legal books, including ground-breaking publications on the law relating to disability equipment provision, to community care, to manual handling in health and social care – and to adult safeguarding (Mandelstam 2013). Of these, the last forms the subject of this piece, with an outline of its development to date and future challenges.

Seeds

In 1987, adult safeguarding – or adult protection as it is sometimes called – was recognised, explicitly and in its own right, neither in policy nor law. By the early 1990s, it had raised its head hesitantly in two publications by the Social Services Inspectorate, then a part of the Department of

Health in England: *Confronting Elder Abuse* (Social Services Inspectorate 1992), and *No Longer Afraid: The Safeguard of Older People in Domestic Settings* (Social Services Inspectorate 1993). During the 1980s and 1990s, child protection would dominate over adult protection just as it continues to do, generally speaking.

Germination

During the 1990s, the realisation grew that adult protection was a very real issue. The Department of Health had missed the boat in 1990 and failed to include any specific provisions in the NHS and Community Care Act of that year, a piece of legislation emphasising the importance of social care assessment of adults in need. By 2000, finally, the Department felt moved to act but appeared too nervous and uncertain about putting anything in law. Instead, it produced statutory guidance called *No Secrets: Guidance on Developing and Implementing Multi-Agency Policies and Procedures to Protect Vulnerable Adults from Abuse* (Department of Health 2000).

The strength of this guidance lay in its official recognition of adult protection and the resulting much-increased levels of safeguarding activity. Its weakness was that it was not law and did little to explain how it related to existing community care legislation. Consequently, for the next 15 years, the legal foundation of adult safeguarding remained muddy and – despite all the valuable and well-intentioned work of local authorities – subject to uncertainties about its legal extent and limits.

Flowering

Convinced of a need for bolder action, the Scottish Parliament stole a march and passed the Adult Support and Protection (Scotland) Act 2007, with explicit definitions and powers of intervention. Lagging behind, the Care Act 2014 finally put adult safeguarding in England onto a statutory footing, although with less clarity and conviction, and with fewer legal powers than in Scotland. The Social Services and Well-Being (Wales) Act 2014 also contains adult safeguarding provisions, with Welsh local authorities being given greater legal powers (in particular, a power of entry) than English, but less than Scottish, authorities.

A future legal issue in safeguarding, at least in England and to some extent Wales, is whether further legislation is needed to give local authorities some sort of coercive power of entry and protection in relation to vulnerable adults who may have mental capacity but who are believed to be unable to make decisions freely for reasons such as undue influence, coercion, duress or threat. This would be in addition to other existing legislative provisions which can in some circumstances be associated with a power of entry under, for example, the Mental Capacity Act 2005, Mental Health Act 1983, Police and Criminal Evidence Act 1983 (section 17: police power of entry) and Public Health Act 1936 (environmental health).

Fruition

Focusing on England, there seems little doubt that the past 17 years has seen a much greater awareness within local authorities – and to some extent other statutory services, as well as independent health and social care providers – about the importance of safeguarding adults from abuse or neglect. Staff are now trained how to recognise different forms of abuse and neglect, and local authorities have detailed policies and procedures in relation to raising alerts, making enquiries and involving other agencies.

Persistent blight and the future

That said, there remain challenges for the future.

- *Statutory basis.* Having operated safeguarding adult procedures for so long with an unclear statutory basis, local authorities are still working towards adherence to the Care Act 2014. For instance, the definition of safeguarding used in some local authorities (protection from harm) is not in line with the Care Act's language (protection from abuse and neglect). Some authorities continue to conduct what they call 'non-statutory' enquiries (meaning outside legislation), without seeming to consider first the various options under the Care Act for protecting people from abuse or neglect.[1]

    Likewise, many have not yet become aware of the duty in sections 6 and 7 of the Care Act of co-operation between statutory services, which is highly relevant to safeguarding. Additionally, new rights of informal carers seem at present to be more paper-based than substance, which may mean that the care they provide may – as a result of physical and mental stress – sometimes become unintentionally

---

1   For example, relevant sections of the Care Act 2014, ss.1, 6, 7, 9, 10, 11, 13, 18, 42, and under the Care and Support (Eligibility) Regulations 2015.

neglectful or abusive, giving rise to wholly avoidable safeguarding concerns.

- *Mental capacity.* In a similar vein, local authorities continue to struggle sometimes to adhere to the basic principles of the Mental Capacity Act, with disastrous effects in some instances on the person (and their family) whom the local authority believes it is 'safeguarding'. Indeed, despite persistent judicial warnings, local authorities, in total good faith, can end up acting coercively and beyond their legal powers and remit.[2]

- *Making safeguarding personal.* Many local authorities use the non-statutory mantras of 'making safeguarding personal' and 'proportionality' (Department of Health 2016, paras 14.3–14.14). The former term means treating the person on an individual basis and not as an object to be passed through the local authority safeguarding process. The latter refers to ensuring that interventions are proportionate to the safeguarding issue and that sledgehammers are not taken to crack nuts. However, 'making safeguarding lawful' might in the future be a more helpful phrase since safeguarding would anyway be both personal and proportionate if conducted in line with the provisions of the Care Act 2014, Mental Capacity Act 2005 (particularly sections 1 and 4) and the Human Rights Act 1998 (particularly article 8 of the European Convention on Human Rights).

---

2   *Local Authority v A* [2010] EWHC 978 (Fam), paras 66, 96.

- *Low-hanging fruit.* By and large, safeguarding currently operates most comfortably when it is aimed at 'low-hanging fruit': that is, easily identifiable situations and perpetrators, such as villainous family members or neighbours, dishonest individual care workers or poorly run local care homes.[3] And sometimes, too readily (Department of Health 2016, paras 14.40, 14.98), safeguarding takes aim at the struggling informal carer – undertaking a Herculean caring routine, largely unaided – whose care standards are perceived to be lapsing through the sheer scale of the unremitting demands.[4]

- *Elephant in the room.* What becomes more difficult and less comfortable is large-scale neglect. This is the elephant in the room. Sometimes, the larger the scale, the less likely it is that anything will be done – in terms even of acknowledgement, let alone remedy. One need only consider, for example, events at Maidstone and Tunbridge Wells NHS Trust (Healthcare Commission 2007), Stoke Mandeville NHS Trust (Healthcare Commission 2006) and Mid Staffordshire NHS Foundation Trust (Francis 2010, 2013). Deliberate shortcuts and distorted priorities, affecting staffing and care in those hospitals, resulted in many hundreds of deaths, in the last case over a three- to four-year period. In fact, events at Mid Staffordshire only really became known fortuitously, not because of their enormity but because of the exceptional efforts of a group of relatives called 'Cure the NHS'. The chairman of the ensuing independent

---

3   *Davis v West Sussex County Council* [2012] EWHC 2152 (QB).

4   *A London Local Authority v JH* [2011] EWHC 2420 (COP).

and public inquiries, Sir Robert Francis, stated in 2017 that, far from lessons being learnt, a repeat is inevitable because of how the NHS is currently operating (Smyth and Lay 2017).

Similarly, Operation Jasmine, a huge police operation into widespread allegations of neglect in Welsh care homes, resulted in little action (Flynn 2015). This raises the question about the extent to which the criminal offences of wilful neglect and ill treatment now covering both individuals and organisations (corporately) within the Mental Health Act 1983, Mental Capacity Act 2005 and Criminal Justice and Courts Act 2015 will be used, useable or useful in relation to systemic neglect.

• *Conflicts of interest.* Making matters more difficult and challenging still, large-scale poor care and neglect are often intrinsically linked to the very statutory services which are commissioning or delivering the care – local authorities, NHS Trusts and NHS clinical commissioning groups – in hospitals, care homes and people's own homes. Yet these are the same statutory services also charged with a central role in safeguarding and are the lynchpin of local safeguarding adults boards. The potential for conflict of interest is huge, as is illustrated by the ruthless treatment, by the very same NHS organisations with safeguarding responsibilities, of NHS staff who raise concerns about the safety of care being delivered (see, e.g., Hammond and Bousfield 2011).

Conclusion

Adult safeguarding has come a long way since 1987 both legally and in practice. Many vulnerable people have benefited from enquiries and interventions made under its banner. And yet, one would surmise that it has a long way to go: first, in terms of applying the basic principles of three key pieces of legislation: the Care Act, Mental Capacity Act and Human Rights Act; and, second, in dealing with the elephant in the room, the institutional poor care and neglect in our health and social care system.

References

Department of Health (2000) *No Secrets: Guidance on Developing and Implementing Multi-Agency Policies and Procedures to Protect Vulnerable Adults from Abuse.* London: Department of Health.

Department of Health (2016) *Care and Support Statutory Guidance.* London: Department of Health.

Flynn, M. (2015) *In Search of Accountability: A Review of the Neglect of Older People Living in Care Homes Investigated as Operation Jasmine.* Cardiff: Welsh Government.

Francis, R. (Chair) (2010) *Independent Inquiry into Care Provided by Mid Staffordshire NHS Foundation Trust January 2005–March 2009.* London: The Stationery Office.

Francis, R. (Chair) (2013) *Report of the Mid Staffordshire NHS Foundation Trust Public Inquiry.* London: The Stationery Office.

Hammond, P. and Bousfield, A. (2011) 'Shoot the messenger: How NHS whistleblowers are silenced and sacked.' *Private Eye,* 22 July.

Healthcare Commission (2006) *Investigation into Outbreaks of Clostridium Difficile at Stoke Mandeville Hospital, Buckinghamshire Hospitals NHS Trust.* London: Healthcare Commission.

Healthcare Commission (2007) *Investigation into Outbreaks of Clostridium Difficile at Maidstone and Tunbridge Wells NHS Trust.* London: Healthcare Commission.

Mandelstam, M. (2013) *Safeguarding Adults and the Law,* second edition. London: Jessica Kingsley Publishers.

Smyth, C. and Lay, K. (2017) 'New NHS scandal is inevitable, Mid Staffs inquiry chief warns.' *The Times,* 10 February.

Social Services Inspectorate (1992) *Confronting Elder Abuse.* London: Department of Health.

Social Services Inspectorate (1993) *No Longer Afraid: The Safeguard of Older People in Domestic Settings.* London: Department of Health.

* * *

MICHAEL MANDELSTAM has provided independent legal training on health and social care for over 20 years. He has written many widely used legal books over the past 30 years, including *Safeguarding Adults and the Law* (second edition, 2013), *Care Act 2014: An A–Z of Law and Practice* (2017) and *Safeguarding Adults: An A–Z of Law and Practice* (forthcoming, 2018), all published by Jessica Kingsley Publishers.

20

30 Years of Service User Involvement and Advocacy

PETER BERESFORD

It is just over 30 years since Suzy Croft and I published the first study of local people's views about social services and user involvement (Beresford and Croft 1986). An enormous amount has happened since that time both in the UK and internationally in terms of user involvement and self-advocacy. Yet what is perhaps both surprising and disappointing is how little real change there has been in social services in line with these developments over that same period. Perhaps the most interesting questions to be asking now, a generation later and with the benefit of hindsight, is why this is so and how it might be altered for the future. Indeed I would suggest that these are central questions to be asking not only in relation to social work and personal services, but also in relation to politics and ideology more generally, both at home in the UK and abroad.

What we have witnessed over most if not all of the 30 years since Jessica Kingsley Publishers came into existence has been a major shift to the right in politics and ideology, both in the UK and internationally. Most often framed in terms of 'neoliberalism', it has meant a trend of cuts in public support services, an increasing political rejection of the values of the post-war welfare states and an uncritical preference for privatisation over state intervention. While the UK has been a leader in this ideological shift, it has also been a global development – over the period globalisation as an economic and political force has been promoted by politicians and economists. Globalisation and neoliberalism have been jointly associated with rising poverty and inequality, between North and South internationally, as well as within nations like the UK. It has been accompanied by massive increases in the amount of enforced population movement created both by large-scale conflict and economic difficulties. In the 2000s the combination of a global economic crash in tandem with increased population movement has led to an increasing right-wing populist emphasis highlighting problems with immigration and refugees, competing for ever-reducing welfare support and job opportunities. This has added to division, stigma and a growing sense of exclusion.

In tandem with the rise of neoliberalism we have witnessed the emergence and influence of new social movements, such as the women's feminist and black civil rights movement, the LGBT liberation movement, and the environmental and peace movements.

Also emerging, but less often discussed and of no less importance, has been the development of new social movements of welfare service users. This has been a global phenomenon and it has included social movements comprising disabled people, mental health service users/ survivors, older people, children and young people looked after by the state, and people living with HIV/AIDS and other long-term conditions. These movements have developed their own innovative 'user-led' or 'user-controlled' organisations (ULOs) which have challenged paternalist attitudes and ways of working shared by traditional charities and voluntary organisations, and social policy prescriptions and welfare systems from the left of centre (Fabian) and right (neoliberal). Such a Fabian approach, which underpinned the post-war UK welfare state, has been based on a narrow group of self-defined professional 'experts' advancing policies they see as progressive but generally with minimal involvement from those they most affect.

The emerging ULOs, with their emphasis on people being able to speak for themselves, have brought about major changes in both public and political understandings of the groups they constitute, highlighting the barriers and discrimination they face rather than the dependence that has traditionally been emphasised. While it is important not to over-state their achievements because of the political and economic obstacles they continue to encounter, they have undoubtedly brought about major policy and practice changes internationally, reflected for example in the United Nations Declaration on the Rights of Disabled Persons (UNDRDP).

One of the ironies of these two very different developments – the shift to neoliberalism and the emergence of welfare user movements – is that they have frequently employed a shared rhetoric, using a common language to mean very different things. This has been particularly true of their shared language of 'user involvement' and 'empowerment'. While the neoliberal model is grounded in principles drawn from consumerism and managerialism, framed very much in terms of the individual having the rights of a 'customer' in their dealings with the state and public services, the version advanced by service user rights organisations is based on the democratisation of policy and services in line with citizens' civil and human rights.

While these different meanings attributed to common terms have caused confusion, it does not take much reflection to understand the difference – to see that a vision based on the 'customer as king' bears little relation to one whose starting point is the democratic rights of people to be treated with equality.

You could argue parallels with this confusion over participative rhetoric in an increasingly deregulated market to theorise the roots of both the Brexit vote in the UK and the election of Donald Trump as US President: we see many disempowered, excluded, impoverished people apparently supporting the very forces of reaction, division and inequality that seem to have oppressed them in the first place. Right-wing populism can seem to have taken the ground from popular aspirations for social justice and collective action. Yet the results of the June 2017 General Election, with an unexpected increase in the Labour vote, associated with calls for the old welfare state values, suggests that this is a struggle that may be far from over.

There is little question that the slow progress in advancing all the bottom-up ideas and developments underpinning user involvement and self-advocacy is linked to the de-funding and marginalisation of public services, especially social support and welfare benefit services, and the negative stereotyping and 'othering' of groups like benefit claimants and refugees by dominant media and political institutions. However, the terrible tragedy of the Grenfell Tower fire has made clear that even this situation can change, when the consequences of such policies become highly visible and previously ignored grassroots campaigning commands attention.

To challenge the anti-welfare direction of travel that until very recently has seemed unstoppable, we need to learn from those who have fought for truly participative and empowering policy and practice: service users and their allies. They have much to tell us, both about what these might look like and how they may be achieved, and there is a rich body of literature summarising what can work.

We have detailed evidence-based studies which offer help in developing participative professional practice based on what service users themselves have to say (Beresford, Adshead and Croft 2007). We can draw on:

- ideas and initiatives that have enabled effective user involvement in research (Beresford and Carr 2012)

- user-led models for person-centred support or 'personalisation' and bottom-up models of change to make it possible (Beresford *et al.* 2011)

- route maps for achieving user involvement in mental health support and services (Weinstein 2009)

- guidance on making partnerships with service users and advocacy groups work (Martin and Gosling 2012)

- books which explain how to support people to have an effective voice through independent advocacy, even where their rights may be at risk (Newbigging *et al.* 2015).

And perhaps most importantly, service user movements have highlighted the importance of giving equal value to experiential as well as traditional professional or 'expert' knowledge – the knowledge people gain from experiencing problems first-hand, 24/7, and of involving people in all their diversity, rather than just the relatively advantaged 'usual suspects' (Beresford 2013, 2016).

These have not been easy times to take forward user involvement and advocacy, but over the past 30 years we have seen evidence increase, knowledge grow and practical projects mushroom. More and more people have become part of this liberatory project. It continues to face resistance, but it can now be seen as at the vanguard of bigger struggles for rights, equality and social justice, and more and more we have the tools to do the job.

References

Beresford, P. (2013) *Beyond the Usual Suspects: Towards Inclusive User Involvement*. Research Report. London: Shaping Our Lives.

Beresford, P. (2016) *All Our Welfare: Towards Participatory Social Policy*. Bristol: Policy Press.

Beresford, P. and Carr, S. (eds) (2012) *Service Users, Social Care and User Involvement* (Research Highlights Series). London: Jessica Kingsley Publishers.

Beresford, P. and Croft, S. (1986) *Whose Welfare: Private Care or Public Services?* Brighton: Lewis Cohen Urban Studies Centre at the University of Brighton.

Beresford, P., Adshead, L. and Croft, S. (2007) *Palliative Care, Social Work and Service Users: Making Life Possible*. London: Jessica Kingsley Publishers.

Beresford, P., Fleming, J., Glynn, M., Bewley, C. *et al.* (2011) *Supporting People: Towards a Person-Centred Approach*. Bristol: Policy Press.

Martin, J. and Gosling, J. (2012) *Making Partnerships with Service Users and Advocacy Groups Work*. London: Jessica Kingsley Publishers.

Newbigging, K., Ridley, J., McKeown, M., Sadd, J. *et al.* (2015) *Independent Mental Health Advocacy: The Right to Be Heard. Context, Values and Good Practice*. London: Jessica Kingsley Publishers.

Weinstein, J. (ed.) (2009) *Mental Health: Service User Involvement and Recovery*. London: Jessica Kingsley Publishers.

* * *

PETER BERESFORD OBE is Professor of Citizen Participation at the University of Essex, co-chair of Shaping Our Lives, the national disabled people's and service users' organisation and network, and Emeritus Professor of Social Policy at Brunel University London. He is a long-term user of mental health services and has a longstanding background of involvement in issues of participation as writer, researcher, activist and teacher. His latest book is *All Our Welfare: Towards Participatory Social Policy* (Policy Press, 2016) and in 2018 Policy Press are publishing *Social Policy First Hand: An International Introduction to Participatory Social Welfare*, jointly edited with Sarah Carr.

21

The Evolving Sounds of Music Therapy

GRACE WATTS

Throughout history, music has been considered a form of healing, with its unique qualities transcending language, culture and geography. As far back as 400 BCE, Hippocrates is said to have played music for his patients with what we would describe today as mental ill health. We have a rich and fascinating historical collection of accounts of the ways in which music and sound were used across cultures to heal, and support health and wellbeing.

Music therapy, as a profession, began to emerge simultaneously in the US and the UK following the Second World War. In the foreword to Darnley-Smith and Patey's seminal text *Music Therapy*, published in 2003, they suggest the evolution of the profession is shaped by clear phases: the early years (1958–1976), which involved setting up the profession; the second phase (1976–1990), which could be described as the professionalisation years; and a third phase as a period of consolidation (1990–2003). I would suggest that the third phase continued until 2011, when the fourth phase began with the merger of the British Society for Music Therapy and the Association for Professional Music Therapists.

We pick up the history in the late 1980s, after the early coming together of the profession in the UK in the 1950s and 1960s, during which the Society for Music Therapy and Remedial Music was formed (later reorganised as the British Society for Music Therapy (BSMT)). From this, the first music therapy training course was established at the Guildhall School of Music and Drama. The tempo of development was rapid over the next 20 years, with several seminal texts published, the drawing together of practitioners through the formation of the Association for Professional Music Therapists (APMT) in 1976, further training courses founded, music therapy posts created and established across the UK, and research developing apace alongside practice.

Nineteen eighty-seven was a significant year of geographical development across the UK for the profession, with formal representation being established in Scotland and music therapy emerging in Northern Ireland. Research was beginning to take centre stage: the third research conference was held, which explored new techniques in collecting data using technology, and was perhaps indicative of the route practitioners were beginning to take in their approaches in exploring how service users could have a voice in their music therapy through self-evaluation. Alongside this, there was a significant development in how research was published: the APMT and BSMT merged their publications to create the *Journal of British Music Therapy*.

The year 1991 marked the sounding of a significant new movement for music therapy: an application was made to the Council for Professions Supplementary to Medicine

(CPSM) for state registration for music therapists. Music therapy was formally ratified in 1996, resulting in music therapists being regulated by the CPSM. Today this body is the Health and Care Professions Council (HCPC) which currently regulates 16 professions, including art therapy and dramatherapy.

By its very nature, music is communicative and collaborative. As the practice of music therapy has developed across continents, communication and collaboration have brought the many sounds of music therapy cultures together. In 1992, the European Music Therapy Conference was held at Kings College, Cambridge, drawing together music therapists from 23 countries. The most recent World Federation for Music Therapy Conference, hosted in Japan in July 2017, was possibly the largest ensemble of music therapists gathering to date, with over 2800 music therapists from 49 countries attending – something that would have been unimaginable 30 years ago!

Collaboration in practice and research has always been a central principle of music therapy regardless of model or approach. International hubs of research such as Aalborg University in Denmark, the Grieg Academy Music Therapy Research Centre, Norway, and the Music Therapy Centre at Anglia Ruskin University, Cambridge, attract music therapists from all over the world to further our understanding of practice and research, facilitating and enabling music therapists to articulate the what, why and how of their speciality beyond their own sound chambers.

Multi-disciplinary working was the focus for the 1995 conference, and this remains a dominant theme in current practice, with music therapists collaborating with colleagues from across health, social care and education, as well as third and private sectors. Collaboration has been instrumental in shaping how models of practice and research have developed to reflect changing needs, and inform and shape knowledge and understanding. Most significantly, collaboration with service users and their carers has helped music therapy to modulate into new sound worlds where its benefits and value can be heard and understood more fully, by a much wider audience.

Throughout the late 1990s and early 2000s, the profile of music therapy continued to evolve: music therapists worked to develop their professional status as recognised allied health professionals, training opportunities were expanded with new courses established, and links continued to be fostered with the profession internationally. Training in other areas of practice was beginning to find a voice, such as guided imagery and neurologic music therapy (NMT), with the first international training for NMT established in 2009.

The year 2012 marked another change in music therapy's evolving sound when the BSMT and APMT merged to form the British Association for Music Therapy (BAMT). The coming together of these two organisations has provided renewed energy for the profession, with the organising of conferences, awareness weeks and a greater contribution to the wider understanding and profile of music therapy.

The music therapy profession has almost doubled in size over the last decade, with over 1000 HCPC-registered music therapists working across the UK with people with extensive varieties of needs, across the lifespan, located in a diverse range of settings. Based on trends of registration with the HCPC, this pattern could potentially repeat itself by 2026 (Sandford 2016).

The dawn of the digital age has enabled music therapists to be amplified in their attempts to be heard and recognised for the contribution they can make to care, health and wellbeing. The migration of the *British Journal of Music Therapy* to an online platform in 2016 has positioned it alongside other leading international music therapy journals. Practice has also been influenced, with new technologies being incorporated into the skills repertoire, providing new channels of accessing music for those who are unable to access traditional music-making methods due to a disability, injury or impairment.

Social media has not only enabled information to flow more freely, but the sharing of practice, research, developments and experiences has provided ways for people to gain further understanding of this discipline, which can look and sound so different depending on context. It has also provided music therapists, both in the UK and internationally, with a platform from which to communicate the how and what of what they do and attempt to answer the inevitable, predestined question, 'What is music therapy?', through myriad universally accessible channels. The answers to this will continue to evolve as needs and context change, but the focus will be for music therapists to continue to find meaningful and relevant ways of articulating what music therapy is, and its impact and value for those who could benefit from it.

Within multi-disciplinary work, music therapy is often described as the golden thread stitching care together. The recent publication of the All-Party Parliamentary Group inquiry report into the arts, health and wellbeing, published in July 2017 (All-Party Parliamentary Group 2017a), recognises the powerful contribution music therapy can bring to our health and wellbeing. It is hoped that this report will encourage those influencing, commissioning and funding services to:

> accept that the arts can make a significant contribution to addressing a number of the pressing issues faced by our health and social care systems… [A]rts-based approaches can help people to stay well, recover faster, manage long-term conditions and experience a better quality of life. (All-Party Parliamentary Group 2017b)

There is no doubt that music therapy will continue to evolve over the next 30 years, but what won't have changed is music therapists' wish to help improve quality of life using the powerful language we all share: music.

References

All-Party Parliamentary Group on Arts, Health and Wellbeing (2017a) 'Creative Health: The Arts for Health and Wellbeing.' www.artshealthandwellbeing.org.uk/appg-inquiry (accessed 12 August 2017).

All-Party Parliamentary Group on Arts, Health and Wellbeing (2017b) 'Creative Health: The Arts for Health and Wellbeing. The Short Report.' www.artshealthandwellbeing.org.uk/appg-inquiry/Publications/Creative_Health_The_Short_Report.pdf (accessed 12 August 2017).

Darnley-Smith, R. and Patey, H. M. (2003) *Music Therapy*, first edition. London: Sage Publications.

Sandford, S. (2016) 'Music Therapists marching, running and playing with the beat.' *British Journal of Music Therapy 30*, 2, 57–64.

* * *

GRACE WATTS has worked for the British Association for Music Therapy (formerly APMT) for over seven years. Alongside this role, she is also a music therapist working in a child development service within the NHS. Grace has worked in a variety of educational settings and adult mental health settings. As part of her current clinical post, she is exploring how music therapy can play a supportive role within maternity services for women, their families, and staff.

22

Developments in Art Therapy Over the Past 30 Years

MARIAN LIEBMANN

Thinking about art therapy 30 years ago feels like visiting another country. Art therapy has grown from a little-known minority pursuit to a well-recognised mainstream form of treatment for many client groups.

Some of the changes reflect wider changes in society. In the 1980s many large, old hospitals closed and their clients resettled in small shared houses in the community. While some of the changes were welcomed, resources in the community were often lacking, and many of those who had been in mental health institutions were unable to cope in the community, and can now often be found in prisons, where many inmates suffer from mental health problems.

Art therapy had been based mainly in hospitals, but then followed clients into the community. Our local group planned a book discussing the change, but gave it up on the realisation that the change was already a fait accompli. Instead we wrote about art therapy in day hospitals and the community (*Art Therapy in Practice*; Liebmann 1990).

Since 1998, art therapy has been statutorily regulated by what was the Council for Professions Supplementary to Medicine (CPSM) and is now the Health and Care Professions Council (HCPC). The titles 'art therapist' and 'art psychotherapist' became protected by law, and anyone wishing to practise in the UK as an art therapist/ art psychotherapist has to be registered with the HCPC. In 1987, there were around 500 British Association of Art Therapists (BAAT) members UK-wide – BAAT being the professional body for UK art therapists. There are currently 2093 HCPC-registered art therapists, of which 1632 are BAAT members (BAAT membership is not a statutory requirement).

Along with the change in registration, art therapists' qualifications have become postgraduate MA degrees, two years full time or three years part time. The number of qualifying courses has increased from three in 1987 to ten training courses now. Some courses have shut for lack of funding, while others have started – there are now courses at the universities of Roehampton, Hertfordshire, Goldsmiths, Chester, Derby, Newport, Sheffield, Edinburgh, Cork and the Institute of Arts in Education in London.

Thirty years ago art therapists were mostly linked with occupational therapy departments in hospitals. This often led to confusion of art therapy with occupational therapy, to the detriment of both. Now the links are more likely to be with psychology or psychotherapy – this is more appropriate, but there are also workplaces where there are enough arts therapists (visual art, drama, dance-movement, music) to form independent departments. However, there has been a recent move towards restructuring services where people work across several areas and no longer belong to departments or teams.

A BAAT workforce survey in 2013 (BAAT 2013a, 2013b) showed that the NHS is no longer the main employer of art therapists. A growing number of art therapists now work in schools, mostly primary, but also some in secondary schools. This is a response to increased demand from schools advised to devote resources to the emotional wellbeing of children following advice from the Department for Education (2016) to ensure good mental health and emotional wellbeing for all pupils.

The other increased demand for art therapy practice has been from voluntary organisations, including those involved in children's counselling, cancer care and hospice care, those working with physical illnesses and neurological conditions, and those supporting refugees. In Calais, art therapists have offered their services to refugees waiting, often destitute, for news of any possible resettlement.

Research has played an increasing role in art therapy. There is now a sizeable cohort of art therapists with PhDs, and there are many interesting research projects in progress. Some examples include: work with grassroots organisations in South Africa, work with older adults and new mothers, uses of art therapy approaches in organisations, work with service users as co-researchers and the development of audio-image recordings (AIRs) as records of work involving service users. With the increasing demand for evidence-based practice, there is much discussion of suitable outcome measures for art therapy, as the commonly used verbal measures do not take account of the visual aspect of art therapy.

As the discipline has grown, BAAT has also expanded its activities considerably. Since 2009, it has prioritised art therapy research and has supported the Art Therapy Practice Research Network (ATPRN), as well as funding a research officer post. It publishes *Newsbriefing*, a biannual newsletter, and has developed a peer-review process to increase the research rating of its journal, *The International Journal of Art Therapy: Inscape*, which has attracted an increase in international submissions. There is now also an online art therapy journal, *ATOL: Art Therapy OnLine*, which receives contributions from art therapists from many countries.

BAAT has also launched initiatives such as the Dual Experience Group, a group for art therapists who have a dual identity as professionals and mental health service users, as they have much to contribute to our understanding of good art therapy practice and research.

Not all the changes in art therapy have been seen as beneficial. Many art therapists, especially in the public sector, now spend more time with computers than with clients, and the 'target culture' often focuses on things that can be measured. Art therapy is difficult to measure simply and easily, owing to its complex structure – more sophisticated methods are needed. There has also been a growth of generic posts in which an art therapist contributes to the general work of a team, for example in therapeutic and risk assessments, as well as providing art therapy, which can sometimes mean that art therapy is squeezed out. On the positive side, this has also opened the door for art therapists who wish to develop general leadership skills and become managers, providing opportunities for career development.

The growth in art therapy in the UK reflects developments elsewhere in the world. The European Consortium for Arts Therapies Education (ECArTE) holds a conference every two years, each time at a different venue in Europe. This conference has gone from strength to strength, attracting delegates from all over the globe.

In the US, the American Art Therapy Association represents nearly 5000 professional art therapists and others related to the art therapy profession (American Art Therapy Association 2017). The Canadian Art Therapy Association is aiming to be a stronger voice for art therapists, bringing them together across the provinces (Canadian Art Therapy Association 2016). ANZATA started in 1987 as the professional association for arts therapy in Australia, and has now expanded to encompass New Zealand and Singapore (ANZATA 2017).

Finally, the theory and research upon which art therapy is based has developed significantly over the past 30 years and will continue to evolve in the future. The standard model of art therapy used 30 years ago was informed by psychoanalysis, but this has broadened to include many other approaches. Art therapists now use gestalt methods, narrative therapy, cognitive theories, cognitive-analytic therapy, developmental theories and family work, to name but a few. Technology is also impacting on art therapy. Art therapists working with young people are developing the use of digital media such as mobile phones and iPads in art therapy.

Work on neuroscience is beginning to provide insights as to why art therapy can be particularly helpful for certain conditions. BAAT is particularly interested in attachment theories, and holds an annual conference on 'Attachment and the Arts'.

It is clear that art therapy has come a long way in the past 30 years. From a little-known minority pursuit, it has grown to be a well-recognised means of helping people in mental distress, especially where words are limited. Its use for people with physical illnesses is also being explored. Research has explored many aspects of the process, with promising developments in neuroscience enlarging our perspective. As art therapists are exploring new theories, there is also a sense of excitement around new practices and new client groups. It will be interesting to see what the next 30 years will achieve.

References

American Art Therapy Association (2017) 'National Staff.' https://arttherapy.org/national-staff (accessed 18 July 2017).

ANZATA (2017) 'About ANZATA.' https://www.anzata.org/About (accessed 18 July 2017).

BAAT (2013a) *BAAT England, Wales & Northern Ireland Workforce Survey.* London: BAAT.

BAAT (2013b) *BAAT Scotland Workforce Survey.* London: BAAT.

Canadian Art Therapy Association (2016) 'Fact Sheet and Advocacy Information.' Available via https://cata15.wildapricot.org/about-art-therapy (accessed 18 July 2017).

Department for Education (2016) *Mental Health and Behaviour in Schools: Departmental Advice for School Staff.* London: Department for Education.

Liebmann, M. (ed.) (1990) *Art Therapy in Practice.* London: Jessica Kingsley Publishers.

* * *

MARIAN LIEBMANN qualified as an art therapist in 1979 and worked in art therapy with offenders, with women's groups and community groups, and for 19 years in the Inner City Mental Health Team in Bristol, where she developed work on anger and also worked with asylum seekers and refugees. She has lectured on art therapy at universities in the UK, Ireland and other European countries. She also works in restorative justice, mediation and conflict resolution, and has used these skills to inform her art therapy work. She has run Art, Conflict and Anger workshops in many countries, including Europe, the US, Latin America and Africa. She has written and edited 12 books, mostly published by Jessica Kingsley Publishers. In 2010 she was awarded her PhD by Publications from Bristol University, and in 2013 she was awarded an OBE for her contribution to social justice through art therapy and mediation. She now undertakes supervision and travels widely for workshops and conferences.

23

Using a Functional Nutrition Approach

LORRAINE NICOLLE

Arriving at her initial consultation, Juliet was keen to talk about her persistent fatigue and 'brain fog'. If she could just get more energy, she said, her life would be transformed. During our discussion, it soon became apparent that other symptoms were also prevalent: bloating after eating, recurrent headaches, an itchy skin rash and daily anxiety, partly due to her fear of developing diabetes as there was a strong family history. Juliet was carrying too much weight around her midriff but was finding it hard to control her eating patterns because of 'unbearable' cravings for sugars and starches. She relied on coffee to keep her going at work and felt too tired to exercise regularly. She used medicated cream for her skin and was considering her GP's suggestion of antidepressants.

With so many symptoms presenting simultaneously, how can we, as healthcare practitioners, know where to start? How do we decide on the best ways in, those crucial points of leverage that would help the patient the most? And how do we know how best to *prioritise* our interventions?

In answer, this is where the 'functional' model of patient care can be so transformative. Developed in the 1980s by the Institute for Functional Medicine in Washington, US, the functional model of healthcare takes the focus away from the symptoms alone and towards investigations of what might be *causing* the symptoms. While a conventional healthcare approach might involve asking, 'What disease does the patient have?', a functional practitioner wants to know 'What sort of individual has the disease?'

Juliet's profile above is a mere scratch on the surface of the in-depth case history that was taken at the consultation in order to start the detective work of identifying the likely antecedents, triggers and mediators that have culminated in her current state of ill health. Such a start-point gives practitioners a far better chance of catalysing long-lasting, even life-changing, results – not just in terms of improving the patient's declared symptoms, but also in helping the patient experience new feelings of 'optimal wellness' they didn't know were possible.

So what exactly is functional nutrition?

The functional approach to patient care is characterised by six basic principles (see the box further below). Much of the model's value is in its focus on the key physiological imbalances that appear to drive degenerative disease. These imbalances include:

- gastro-intestinal disturbances like dysbiosis (changes in the balance of microbes in the gut) and intestinal hyperpermeability (otherwise known as 'leaky gut')

- poor hepatic biotransformation (detoxification processes), including problems with methylation

(a particular biochemical pathway involved not only in detoxification, but also brain chemistry, immune function, healthy cell division and even the way in which genes function: methylation is known as an 'epigenetic' process, which helps to control which of our genes are turned on, and which stay silent)

- dysglycaemia and dyslipidaemia (problems with controlling the metabolism of sugars and fats, respectively)

- endocrine (that is, hormonal) imbalances, including adrenal, thyroid and sex hormones

- immune system dysregulation and inflammation

- compromised essential fatty acid metabolism (that is, the way in which fats from foods are converted into healthy versus problematic chemicals in the body)

- poor energy production and increased oxidative stress (in which reactive molecules called free radicals can damage cells and our DNA)

- dysregulated neurotransmitter function (or problems with balancing brain chemistry)

- structural problems like collagen degradation that affects bones, muscles, joints, skin and mucous membranes.

Most of today's chronic illnesses, such as cardiovascular disease, cancer, diabetes, mental health problems and autoimmunity, tend to be preceded by years of reduced function in one or more of the body processes above. Moreover, many patients come to us not because they have a named medical condition but because, like Juliet, they are suffering myriad chronic, debilitating symptoms, involving various different organ systems, but which don't always have any discernible organic cause. In functional nutrition terms, this does not make the patient's health conditions any less 'real', nor any less concerning if one is looking to minimise her risk for developing chronic diseases in her middle and later years.

THE PRINCIPLES OF FUNCTIONAL MEDICINE

- An understanding of the biochemical individuality of each patient

- A patient-centred versus a disease-centred approach

- The search for a dynamic balance among internal and external factors

- Familiarity with the web-like interconnections of internal physiological factors

- Seeing 'health' as not merely the absence of disease, but as a positive vitality

- The promotion of organ reserve for a healthy old age.

Adapted from Jones 2005, p.6

Making links between signs/ symptoms and causes

Key to the success of any functional intervention plan is the ability to see ways in which such imbalances may be linked to clinical signs and symptoms. This guides the practitioner in where and how to intervene, in knowing which body systems need more support. In most cases, each of the clinical imbalances listed above has the potential to be altered so as to improve the function of the body's cells and organs, and ultimately improve signs and symptoms of ill health, whether or not these are part of a named medical condition. Imbalances in the gut, for example, are now increasingly acknowledged as drivers of *systemic* symptoms and even some diseases, including some autoimmune diseases, obesity and associated metabolic changes, and some mental health issues.

Is this an evidence-based approach to healthcare?

In the medical world, a functional approach is still a minority paradigm. But it is practised by all registered nutritional therapists in the UK and is based on well-respected disciplines like molecular biology and nutrition science, while also drawing on some of the most exciting emerging sciences like systems biology (looking at the function of systems in the body, rather than their molecules, cells and other individual component parts in isolation) and nutri-epigenetics (how food nutrients affect our health through their ability to change how our genes behave).

Work in the field of epigenetics teaches us that the balance of health and disease is not so much driven by our genetic *inheritance*, but by environmental factors triggering gene *expression* (the term used to describe a gene being activated to do something in the body). Our lifestyles, diets and dietary supplements are important environmental triggers. Dietary practices like calorie restriction, fasting and time-restricted feeding, for example, have powerful effects on health via epigenetic mechanisms. And there is a fast-growing body of evidence for individual nutrients exerting many of their effects through their influence on genetic expression. A helpful metaphor for epigenetic processes was provided by *National Geographic* in 2012:

> If you think of our DNA as an immense piano keyboard and our genes as keys – each key symbolizing a segment of DNA responsible for a particular note, or trait, and all the keys combining to make us who we are – then epigenetic processes determine when and how each key can be struck, changing the tune being played. (Miller 2012)

Such nutrients include vitamins A and D, omega-3 fish oils and many chemicals found in plants – 'phytochemicals' – such as curcumin from the turmeric root, resveratrol from grapes, genistein from soy beans and a compound called EGCG from green tea.

The power of personalised plans

Another key value of the functional approach is its focus on *personalised* programmes. In its bid to improve dietary adequacy in the UK, the Department of Health sets a reference nutrient intake (RNI) for micronutrients to specify what everyone in the population needs for health. In sharp contrast to this, award-winning researchers in the field of human biochemistry and medicine, such as Professor Robert Heaney MD and Professor Bruce Ames, believe that such systems are inadequate because they fail to take account of *individual* needs.

Ames (2002) found that as many as a third of all our genetic variations reduce the effectiveness of cofactor (micronutrient) binding sites. In other words, we are genetically different in the ability of our biological processes to grab hold of food nutrients and use them to do things that keep us healthy. This implies that, for normal functioning, certain individuals may need these nutrients at far higher levels than the standard RNIs, and that they'll need a lot more than individuals without the genetic variations.

Nutritional insufficiency and disease

Researchers like Ames and Heaney go even further, by saying that the government-recommended intake levels are probably too low for *everyone*. This is because they are designed to prevent the classic deficiency diseases like scurvy and beriberi, also known as thiamine deficiency. They do not take into account the insidious biochemical consequences of chronic insufficiencies of a more moderate order. In other words, they don't acknowledge that even a slight reduction in a nutrient over the long term can cause problems in the body that develop so slowly that they can go unnoticed until it is too late, that is, until the problem has progressed into a disease.

In 2006 Ames proposed his 'triage' theory to explain how even such modest insufficiencies are common causes of many types of chronic disease (Ames 2006). He proposed that these modest shortfalls, common in the population, trigger a 'triage' response such that metabolic functions critical to short-term survival (e.g. energy production) are favoured by the body at the expense of functions needed for longer-term health, such as the prevention of DNA damage. Thus he proposed that optimal (and personalised) intakes of micronutrients are crucial in reducing society's burgeoning problem of age-related diseases.

The journey

I have provided a broad overview of where we have come from and where we currently stand in the field of functional nutrition, but it's time to get back to Juliet. How will her road to better health be revealed?

We have established that the detailed elucidation of the life story comes first. Some practitioners find it helpful to plot this in a timeline, indicating the environmental inputs (diet, medications, leisure habits, psychological stressors and others), medical test results and clinical signs and symptoms in blocks of five years or so.

From Juliet's point of view, this is also the start of the healing process, for she finds it cathartic to relate the story of her life. The process also helps her to see her situation more objectively and, perhaps for the first time, to spot connecting threads between her lifestyle and her health issues.

Once the timeline has been drafted, the practitioner arranges for Juliet to undertake any laboratory investigations that she believes will be enlightening. For example, it may be helpful for Juliet to undertake stool, urine and/or breath testing to identify the extent to which any dysfunctions in the gastro-intestinal tract may be affecting her bodywide symptoms, and/or more broad-based tests to get an idea of her functional levels of vitamins, minerals and antioxidants, her toxic load (including toxic metals) and the functioning of her detox systems, adrenal glands and other body processes like those mentioned above.

Information from the case history and the lab tests is then mapped on a 'matrix' diagram in a way that helps to identify which of the body systems are most likely to be in need of support to improve their functioning. In this way, the functional matrix acts as a lens through which the practitioner can spot patterns that enable effective judgements to be made about likely causes and effects, and thus can arrive at the most effective interventions.

This is just the start of the iterative analytical process that will lead the practitioner to devise a long-term strategic plan and periodically set shorter-term action plans for Juliet. She will work in partnership with Juliet, educating her about the links between her diet, lifestyle, biochemical imbalances and clinical symptoms, and motivating her to take responsibility for making the recommended changes.

A discussion of the specific nutritional interventions for Juliet is beyond the scope of this chapter, but the issue of where and how one could intervene in such cases is discussed in greater depth in the author's books *Biochemical Imbalances in Disease* (Nicolle and Woodriff Beirne 2010), *The Functional Nutrition Cookbook* (Nicolle and Bailey 2013) and *Eat to Get Younger* (Nicolle and Bailey 2014), all published by Jessica Kingsley Publishers and their Singing Dragon imprint.

And finally...

Proponents of the functional approach believe that it epitomises the systems-oriented, personalised intervention that is needed to meet the greatest healthcare challenge of the twenty-first century, that of the sharply rising 'epidemic' of chronic disease. Working functionally is not an *easy* option. But using the framework can bring hitherto unattainable rewards in terms of improving clinical judgement and patient outcomes.

And for those who are yet to be convinced of the power of this approach, it's worth remembering that all disease arises from the interaction of genetic uniqueness with environmental inputs. Hence, how could diet and lifestyle *not* be considered crucial?

Adapted from an article originally published in CAM Magazine (Nicolle 2011).

References

Ames, B. N. (2002) 'High dose vitamin therapy stimulates variant enzymes with decreased coenzyme binding affinity (increased Km): relevance to genetic disease and polymorphisms.' *American Journal of Clinical Nutrition 75*, 616–658.

Ames, B. N. (2006) 'Low micronutrient intake may accelerate the degenerative diseases of aging through allocation of scarce micronutrients by triage.' *Proceedings of the National Academy of Science 103*, 47, 17589–17594.

Jones, D. (2005) *Textbook of Functional Medicine.* Gig Harbor, WA: Institute of Functional Medicine.

Miller, P. (2012) 'A thing or two about twins.' *National Geographic,* January. www.nationalgeographic.com/magazine/2012/01/identical-twins-science-dna-portraits (accessed 26 July 2017).

Nicolle, L. (2011) 'Focusing on functionality: How to get better results in nutritional therapy.' *CAM Magazine 2*, 8. www.lorrainenicollenutrition. co.uk/pdfs/CAM%20Biochem%20Imbals%20article%20April%202011. pdf (accessed 26 July 2017).

Nicolle, L. and Bailey, C. (2013) *The Functional Nutrition Cookbook: Addressing Biochemical Differences Through Diet.* London: Singing Dragon.

Nicolle, L. and Bailey, C. (2014) *Eat to Get Younger: Tackling Inflammation and Other Ageing Processes for a Longer, Healthier Life.* London: Jessica Kingsley Publishers.

Nicolle, L. and Woodriff Beirne, A. (eds) (2010) *Biochemical Imbalances in Disease: A Practitioner's Handbook.* London: Singing Dragon.

* * *

LORRAINE NICOLLE, MSc, mBANT, CNHC, RNT, is an experienced nutrition clinician, educator and author and has been practising nutritional therapy in London since 2003. Using a functional medicine approach, she focuses on helping clients with healthy ageing. Many of her clients have complex, chronic conditions such as autoimmune diseases, low bone density, gastro-intestinal disorders, long-term pain, stress-related conditions or severe fatigue. She also supports clients nutritionally throughout medical treatment for cancer.

Lorraine is a qualified university teacher and has taught on many nutrition and health-related programmes, including at the University of West London and Greenwich University. She also works with a nutritional healthcare company and a medical laboratory, writing and delivering lectures for healthcare practitioners who are keen to further their nutrition knowledge. Lorraine has co-authored three functional nutrition books, all published by Jessica Kingsley Publishers.

See www.lorrainenicollenutrition.co.uk for more information.

24

Occupational Therapy

Everyday Acts Become Our Legacy

WINNIE DUNN

Living life forward is not the same experience as reflecting back on all the life moments that have come before. In the present moment we may experience joy and wonder; we also experience ambiguity and may feel unsure about the meaning of our everyday actions.

When we look back on our lives, we see the coherence that wasn't visible as we stepped through tasks and activities day by day. Looking back reminds us that our actions in the present moment *do* matter, and not just for our peace of mind now; our actions accumulate to become our legacy. We experience this phenomenon of accumulated meaning individually, and we also experience it collectively in our families, communities, professions and culture. The discipline of occupational therapy (OT) is just the same; our small acts have accumulated to a legacy of significant contributions on behalf of the people we serve, their families and even to the lives of the occupational therapy professionals themselves.

Thirty years ago, when Jessica Kingsley Publishers were just getting started in London and had yet to open its own US office (JKP Inc was launched in 2004), occupational therapy in the United States had entered a big growth cycle. For example, from 1970 to 1988 the number of education programs increased from 37 programs serving 720 students nationwide to 64 programs serving 2295 students. Leaders were beginning to talk about graduate education for occupational therapists, thinking that the knowledge base was growing past the capacity possible at the baccalaureate level. The number of professional journals had increased from one to five publications, indicating the correlating expansion of material available to publish about occupational therapy topics (Grant and Labovitz 1989).

Occupational therapy was expanding in practice as well. For example, occupational therapy was included in federal laws as key providers for young children and school-aged children. Therapists were learning that applying 'medical model' strategies in schools and early intervention programs was not useful, and so national leaders wrote guidelines for services in these new settings.

Simultaneously, scholars were calling for a recommitment to core ideas in occupational therapy philosophy. The profession had concentrated on being precise with certain procedures; scholars started writing about what makes life meaningful for people and how to adapt homes and workplaces to support people in their life activities in occupational therapy. There were also discussions about the relationships between theory and practice and how they affect each other, and ways to advance ideas for the profession as a whole.

During the late 1990s and early 2000s, occupational therapy scholars and providers turned their attention to measurement as a way to characterize the profession's ideas. Researchers in OT had developed standardized ways to measure people's performance, which built confidence in occupational therapy's contributions to recovery and development. With more standardized data, it was easier to see OT's impact on people's lives, which fostered more theories about how to be effective in serving others' needs.

Occupational therapy professionals were part of service systems such as hospitals, rehabilitation facilities and schools that expected professionals to validate their work as useful and effective. To meet these demands, scholars and providers worked together to design measurement strategies that would document both current performance and progress during therapy. Occupational therapists began employing advanced measurement and statistical methods to increase validity and reliability of observations and test results. All this measurement work coincided with a move to graduate-level entry into the profession (master's degree). Having a growing body of knowledge and formal ways to write about findings created a significantly larger scope for professionals entering the field. It would take more time to learn the base knowledge, and graduate-level degrees would reflect this more complex thinking that would be necessary for successful practice. There was also a growing number of occupational therapy programs that began offering academic doctoral degrees, paving the way for more formal knowledge development.

This focus on quantitative reporting was balanced with calls for embracing the complexity and 'heart' involved in service to people and families who are vulnerable. Discussions continued about the importance of meaning in people's lives, specifically the meaning they derive from their life activities rather than the meaning professionals might impose from an 'objective' stance.

In the past decade, occupational therapy has taken its rightful place as a mature discipline. There is a call for the entry-level degree to be at the doctoral level, specifically a professional doctorate similar to other professional disciplines like architecture, business and engineering. There is also a significant increase in occupational therapists entering academic doctoral education (PhD or equivalent) to prepare themselves to provide higher education teaching and direct formal research programs. This marks the first generation of occupational therapy students who aspire to an academic/research career from the start. In prior decades academic occupational therapists transitioned from practice or management, having gotten their doctoral degrees in other disciplines. This decade also marks a range of choices for occupational therapists to enter doctoral programs within the discipline.

Interestingly, the burgeoning of ideas has created a return to some themes from earlier decades. Scholars are again writing about conceptual ideas that anchor the profession, and how those ideas show up in the current service environments. For example, there is an emphasis on finding ways to support people within the community, not just when they are in hospitals with acute illness. Therapists spend time in people's employment settings to find out how to make their work more effective, and visit families in their homes to understand the context of their children's lives as they search for the best interventions together. With the advances in communication options, colleagues are collaborating across settings and even across the world to find similarities and differences in applying occupational therapy evidence.

And as we enter Jessica Kingsley Publishers' fourth decade of service to knowledge dissemination, new ideas continue to emerge in the field of occupational therapy. People with various conditions such as autism and their families are speaking up, writing about their experiences, contributing to the literature about how they want to be seen, and expressing what they need from professionals to support them to have a rich and satisfying life.

This new surge of information invites occupational therapy professionals and scholars to reconceptualize how to enact core principles. For example, adult self-advocates (such as people who have autism) are telling us that the sensory aspects of an environment and activity matter to their ability to participate in chosen activities. How will occupational therapists rise to the challenge of making the world friendlier for self-advocates?

Thankfully, Jessica Kingsley Publishers has been making these voices available to us. How will we respond to create the next chapter for occupational therapy? How will Jessica Kingsley Publishers continue to make new voices available? As before, actions taken now will serve as a legacy in the future.

Reference

Grant, H. K. and Labovitz, D. R. (1989) 'Progress in education: 1970–1988.' *American Journal of Occupational Therapy 43*, 193–195.

* * *

WINNIE DUNN, PhD, OTR, FAOTA, is a Distinguished Professor in the Department of Occupational Therapy at the University of Missouri. She is the author of *Living Sensationally: Understanding Your Senses* (Jessica Kingsley Publishers, 2008).

25

Therapeutic Communities

Adapt or Die!

REX HAIGH AND JAN LEES

By 1987, the year that Jessica Kingsley Publishers was founded, therapeutic communities (TCs) in the UK had established themselves as a radical alternative to mainstream psychiatry.

The modern British TC emerged from wartime military experiments and the heat of the 1960s and 1970s 'social psychiatry' movement – a form of psychiatry that focused on the interpersonal and cultural contexts of mental health and illness. The doors of wards were unlocked, and therapeutic communities were firmly against medical orthodoxy – the power invested in hierarchy and status – and the use of physical treatments, such as newly emerging psychotropic medications.

Instead, TCs promoted democracy, empowerment, the treatment of equals by equals and the importance of 'being with' rather than 'doing to'. The main principles included challenge and confrontation in a flattened hierarchy, and a culture of enquiry in which group members felt emotionally contained and sufficiently safe to do the necessary psychological work. In TCs, risk is contained through relationships rather than protocols and procedures.

Although this chapter primarily addresses democratic therapeutic communities for people with mental health difficulties, there is also a diverse and thriving tradition of TC provision for children and young people, particularly in the field of progressive education. There is also a very large worldwide contingent of addiction TCs. Their origins were very different to 'democratic' TCs, yet they have become increasingly similar (Haigh and Lees 2008).

Over the past 30 years, TCs have been effective in adapting and changing in response to challenges, just as their members are expected to do the same in their own lives: changing in response to increasingly austere economic policies, and increasing emphasis on short-termism in public services, and the rise of individualism and consumerism which are the antithesis of TC values and principles.

While the late 1980s and 1990s saw the closure of many residential NHS TCs because of financial constraints, creative adaptations were developed in order to survive. Two new national residential NHS TCs were set up to replicate the work of the Henderson Hospital, which was the direct descendant of the wartime experiments, and became the flagship for democratic therapeutic community practice in the NHS and prisons. Other NHS residential TCs responded to the challenge by converting to non-residential programmes, and a number of day TCs were established as part of the National Personality Disorder Development Programme which ran from 2002 to 2011. Four new TC wings were established as part of a new purpose-built private prison, HMP Dovegate. Researchers in the TC field were awarded two major grants: one to undertake a systematic review of the evidence base in the TC literature and the other for a multicentre comparative research study (Freestone *et al.* 2006; Lees, Evans, Freestone and Manning 2006; Lees, Evans and Manning 2005; Lees, Manning, Menzies and Morant 2004; Lees, Manning and Rawlings 1999, 2004).

A TC book series was founded in 1979 and was revived by Jessica Kingsley Publishers in 1998. The series has in recent years been renamed 'Community, Culture and Change', and has featured 18 new volumes to date through JKP. Another important publication for the TC community during these oscillations in TC fortunes has been *The International Journal of Therapeutic Communities*, which has now published 37 volumes.

In response to increasing government regulation and inspection of care provision in the early 2000s, TCs again responded creatively by devising an international network of peer review and audit, which was based on TC principles: the 'Community of Communities'. It sets its core standards by democratic processes, involves current and ex-service users at all levels, and implements its audits in an inclusive and empowering way (Haigh and Tucker 2004).

More recently, although British TCs continue to struggle to survive in the current political and economic climate, there are still some new and interesting developments in the field. One is the establishment of regular experiential training communities, the 'Living-Learning Experience' workshops, which were run as transient three-day therapeutic communities themselves. These were originally set up to give staff working in therapeutic communities the experience of what it is like to be a member of that therapeutic community. However, they have more recently been adapted for broader use in training for relational practice in groups, teams and organisations. These events have been running in the UK for over 20 years, and the programme and structure is now being faithfully reproduced and used throughout Italy (where it has been used in workshops for entrepreneurs and business leaders), India and Portugal (Lees *et al.* 2016). In Sicily, the government has encouraged the setting up and funding of new TCs, and several Italian centres have also set up networks adapted from the UK's Community of Communities.

In 2007, the Community of Communities started a spin-off project called 'Enabling Environments' (EE). By distilling the underlying relational values from several years of TC audit data, ten standards were set, based on therapeutic community principles and values such as attachment, communication and openness (see www. enablingenvironments.com). These represent the ways in which the therapeutic community ethos and atmosphere is established, but without any of the structural requirements of therapeutic communities, such as community meetings or specially trained staff. They are therefore transposable to a wide range of settings where the quality of relationships is seen as crucial, such as care homes for older people, ecotherapy projects and day centres for learning disabilities.

This work, and the portfolio-based award to which it leads, now underlies new ways of working in the homelessness and prison sectors. Psychologically informed environments (PIEs) are transforming homelessness hostels by introducing practices informed by TC principles and values, while psychologically informed planned environments (PIPEs) are doing the same in prisons and probation premises (Haigh *et al.* 2012). Most recently, all UK 'approved premises' (probation hostels) are being supported to become accredited Enabling Environments, and their use in other public service settings is being explored.

An additional extension of TC and EE practices is seen in 'greencare', in all its forms. This entails including nature and the natural world as an integral part of therapeutic programmes: it can include therapeutic horticulture, animal-assisted interventions, care farming and wilderness camping (Haigh 2012). Engaging in groups for meaningful work activities, seeing and enjoying the products of your labour, and collaborative and non-hierarchical structures are all common to both greencare and TCs.

Therapeutic communities have also had to respond to dogmatic demands for evidence-based practice, and precisely specified interventions. The first response was the publication of the research findings of a modern randomised controlled trial of non-residential therapeutic community treatment for people with personality disorders. It showed various significant improvements over treatment as usual (Pearce *et al.* 2017). The second has been the publication of *A Handbook of Democratic Therapeutic Community Theory and Practice* (Pearce and Haigh 2017) – the first work of its kind to bring together the whole range of theoretical underpinnings, and to demonstrate how these are carried out in modern TC practice.

Although the future remains uncertain, basic TC principles will endure. Democratic involvement in decisions and patient involvement have become mainstream, treating patients with respect and dignity – as human beings with strengths and weaknesses – is now standard practice, and hierarchies are increasingly being flattened. With so many of the early countercultural and progressive ideas of TCs having been taken up and implemented by orthodox services,

TCs will need to continue to change and adapt, in creative and forward-looking ways, to keep their radical edge.

References

Freestone, M., Lees, J., Evans, C. and Manning, M. (2006) 'Histories of trauma in client members of therapeutic communities.' *Therapeutic Communities* 27, 3, 387–409.

Haigh, R. (2012) 'The philosophy of greencare: Why it matters for our mental health.' *Mental Health and Social Inclusion 16*, 3, 127–134.

Haigh, R. and Lees, J. (2008) 'Fusion TCs: Divergent histories, converging challenges.' *Therapeutic Communities 29*, 4, 347–374.

Haigh, R. and Tucker, S. (2004) 'Democratic development of standards: The community of communities – a quality network of therapeutic communities.' *Psychiatric Quarterly 75*, 3, 263–277.

Haigh, R., Harrison, T., Johnson, R., Paget, S. and Williams, S. (2012) 'Psychologically informed environments and the "Enabling Environments" initiative.' *Housing, Care and Support 15*, 1, 34–42.

Lees, J., Evans, C., Freestone, M. and Manning, N. (2006) 'Who comes into therapeutic communities? A description of the characteristics of a sequential sample of client members admitted to 17 therapeutic communities.' *Therapeutic Communities 27*, 3, 411–433.

Lees, J., Evans, C. and Manning, N. (2005) 'A cross-sectional snapshot of therapeutic community client members.' *Therapeutic Communities 26*, 3, 295–314.

Lees, J., Haigh, R., Lombardo, A. and Rawlings, B. (2016) 'Transient therapeutic communities: The "living-learning experience" trainings.' *Therapeutic Communities 37*, 2, 57–68.

Lees, J., Manning, N., Menzies, D. and Morant, N. (2004) *A Culture of Enquiry: Research Evidence and the Therapeutic Community*. London: Jessica Kingsley Publishers.

Lees, J., Manning, N. and Rawlings, B. (1999) *Therapeutic Community Effectiveness: A Systematic International Review of Therapeutic Community Treatment for People with Personality Disorders and Mentally Disordered Offenders*. York: NHS Centre for Reviews and Dissemination.

Lees, J., Manning, N. and Rawlings, B. (2004) 'A culture of enquiry: Research evidence and the therapeutic community.' *Psychiatric Quarterly 75*, 3, 279–294.

Pearce, S. and Haigh, R. (2017) *A Handbook of Democratic Therapeutic Community Theory and Practice*. London: Jessica Kingsley Publishers.

Pearce, S., Scott, L., Attwood, G., Saunders, K. *et al.* (2017) 'Democratic therapeutic community treatment for personality disorder: Randomised controlled trial.' *British Journal of Psychiatry 210,* 2, 149–156.

* * *

Both **REX HAIGH** and **JAN LEES** have been involved in therapeutic community practice, research, training and publishing for many years. Rex is an NHS consultant psychiatrist in medical psychotherapy, and he and Jan Lees are both group analysts. They are both directors of Growing Better Lives, a social enterprise committed to ecotherapy and therapeutic community development.

Rex's publications include *A Handbook of Democratic Therapeutic Community Theory and Practice* (with Steve Pearce; Jessica Kingsley Publishers, 2017), and Jan's include *A Culture of Enquiry: Research Evidence and the Therapeutic Community* (edited with Nick Manning, Diana Menzies and Nicola Morant; Jessica Kingsley Publishers, 2004). They have co-authored the articles 'Transient therapeutic communities: The "living-learning experience" trainings' (with Aldo Lombardo and Barbara Rawlings; 2016) and 'Therapeutic communities and group analysis' (with Sarah Tucker; 2017), both for *The International Journal of Therapeutic Communities.*

26

What Seest Thou Else?

The Past and Future of Forensic Psychotherapy

GWEN ADSHEAD

> *What seest thou else, in the dark backward and abysm of Time?*

> Shakespeare, *The Tempest*

Over 25 years ago, I wrote a short article wondering whether forensic psychotherapists were a 'dying breed or evolving species' (Adshead 1991). As a very junior psychiatrist, I had the privilege of being taught by people like psychoanalyst, prison doctor and forensic psychiatrist Dr Pat Gallwey, and consultant psychotherapist at Broadmoor high security hospital Dr Murray Cox, who used psychodynamic thinking to understand offenders and their offences.

A key component of their psychodynamic frame of reference was the assumption that the offence has meaning for the offender; that it was a communication of some desperate, cruel and brutal message. Therefore, the men and women who commit their offences need psychological therapy to help them and others understand their message, to help them communicate in more pro-social ways, and to explore how they can be safe in the future. Further, a psychodynamic approach helps professionals working with offenders to be ready to hear what they have to say, and not exclude them from human thought and reflection. Finally, psychodynamic approaches to forensic patients are essential for humanising custodial environments, because they can enable forensic professionals and organisations to think better when they themselves are stressed and angry, and thus avoid acting in a way that parallels the offences of their patients.

My earliest teachers had developed their craft in general practice, general psychiatry, psychoanalysis and group analysis, and my short article wondered where the future forensic psychotherapists would come from, and how forensic professionals could learn to bring that psychodynamic language to the sometimes brutal and unthinking discourse that takes place in prisons and secure hospitals. My concern was that it seemed hard to get psychological thinking into these places; that therapy was not routinely offered to offenders and patients who had offended when mentally ill; that the emotional responses of staff sometimes got in the way of delivering good care and led to a lack of reflection on the process; and that there seemed to be little opportunity to train as a therapist as well as being a forensic practitioner. I did not anticipate at all just how fruitful, rich and exciting the subsequent years would be.

First, the International Association of Forensic Psychotherapy (IAFP) was born in 1990. Since then it has grown into a strong and active organisation with members in many countries. The IAFP has recently had its annual conference in Sicily; the next one is in Belfast in 2018. It is now registered as a charity in the UK, which allows it to raise money for research and potentially to offer training opportunities. Consultant forensic psychiatrist Dr Estela Welldon was instrumental in the IAFP's early development, and she also set up a diploma in forensic psychotherapy at the Portman Clinic in London. This course set the foundations for the training of a range of forensic practitioners in psychodynamic thinking, which in turn encouraged the development of new consultant posts in psychotherapy in secure psychiatric hospitals such as Broadmoor and Rampton Hospital.

Next, new training schemes for junior psychiatrists were developed which combined training in both forensic psychiatry and psychotherapy. Anyone who has been involved in education and curriculum development (and psychotherapy training in particular) will know how hard this process can be, and much hard work was done by many forensic psychiatrists and psychotherapists, modelling how this collaboration could work. Forensic psychotherapy training schemes developed all over the UK; not in huge numbers, but enough to develop a culture of thought. A Special Interest Group was set up at the Royal College of Psychiatrists, and quality standards were developed by the Royal College of Psychiatrists which stated that all secure units should have access to a consultant forensic psychotherapist who could support staff by providing reflective practice groups.

Many of the forensic practitioners who became involved with the IAFP or who completed the Portman diploma went on to write interesting and important books about their work, which helped to cement an academic base for forensic psychotherapy. Jessica Kingsley Publishers was crucial to this process, supporting the development of a series of books entitled 'Forensic Focus', which developed and supported authors in writing about forensic psychotherapy. A two-volume textbook in forensic psychotherapy entitled *Forensic Psychotherapy: Crime, Psychodynamics and the Offender Patient* was published in 1996, edited by Murray Cox and Christopher Cordess, and the Forensic Focus series went on to feature a range of volumes about different types of psychotherapeutic work with forensic patients and prisoners: drama therapy, music therapy and therapy with offenders with learning disability; and psychodynamic issues in forensic nursing: over 50 titles that constitute a solid body of practical evidence about the value of psychodynamic thinking in work with offenders. This work supported colleagues in European countries and the US to support psychodynamic thinking in forensic practice.

Finally, forensic psychotherapeutic thinking has been hugely influential in developing organisational thought about work with offenders, both in prisons and secure psychiatric care, especially in relation to the support of staff and their wellbeing. There is recognition that secure services (including prisons) need to provide security that is physical, procedural and relational: that is, that attends to the relationships between staff members and between staff and patients. Secure services need a 'thinking organisational structure' that helps to keep professional minds 'secure', which in turn allows professionals to think in complex ways about the risk that offenders pose, whether this is in the form of dangerous behaviour or risky beliefs about others. Relational security also allows staff to attend to the distress that offenders feel, and the emotional labour of caring for offenders. In the UK, this recognition is at a national policy level and has influenced the development of specialised units in prisons for offenders with personality disorders and attachment problems. The focus in these units is not so much on therapy for offenders, but in helping staff to feel empowered and skilled in how they cope with the emotional costs of their work.

So what lies ahead for forensic psychotherapy? Perhaps inevitably, after many years of growth and rich harvest, we find ourselves in fallow years and in uncertain times. Cuts to UK health services have seen psychotherapy posts cut and not replaced. Anxiety about scarce resources leads to malignant competition between service providers, and attacks on therapies that are seen (erroneously) as being long term and not focused on risk reduction. Psychodynamic thinking also comes under attack because it tolerates uncertainty, ambiguity and loss, which cause fear and alarm in healthcare services that base their business model on industrial manufacture, rather than human services.

The success of forensic psychotherapy has energised other schools of psychological therapists to offer therapies to offenders, such as cognitive behavioural therapy and dialectical behaviour therapy. These therapies also claim to improve mental health and reduce risk, and also claim to be less expensive in terms of time and professional resources. Although these approaches do have strengths and can be highly effective for some aspects of offender mental health, they are insufficient when they only focus on conscious experience and exclude the relational context in which offences take place. It is especially important in the treatment of offenders to include therapies that pay attention to unconscious repetition of childhood attachments, because these often play a part in the genesis of violence and can be repeated in therapeutic relationships; and therapies that focus only on conscious self-report may miss vital information. A focus only on conscious cognitions risks omitting attention to the 'dark matter' of the human heart, which is a potent source of human cruelty.

The best evidence we have suggests that the psychological rehabilitation of offenders requires all types of therapy to be offered at different times in a person's journey, whether in prison or secure services. Such an approach is commonplace in the long-term rehabilitation of physical disorders (for example, after spinal injuries) but sadly, in mental health, commissioners tend to dismiss the idea that multiple different therapies are needed across a lengthy timescale. What is likely to be most useful is a programme of different therapeutic techniques that work in a complementary way, and where no single type of therapy is promoted or excluded.

Keeping hopeful has always been a key aspect of forensic psychotherapy, and anticipation is a mature defence against fear, distress and anger. Although we have lost some wonderful people and services over the years, we have gained a body of knowledge that cannot be undone or forgotten. Given my singular lack of foresight 26 years ago, it would be foolish of me to opine too certainly on what I see in the 'abysm of Time'. But I am hopeful that Jessica Kingsley Publishers will continue to be a part of that future, helping forensic psychotherapists preserve and develop our knowledge, our wisdom and our capacity to think.

References

Adshead, G. (1991) 'The forensic psychotherapist: Dying breed or evolving species?' *Psychiatric Bulletin 15*, 410–412.

Cox, M. and Cordess, C. (eds) (1996) *Forensic Psychotherapy: Crime, Psychodynamics and the Offender Patient* (Forensic Focus). London: Jessica Kingsley Publishers.

* * *

GWEN ADSHEAD is a consultant forensic psychiatrist and psychotherapist. She has worked in secure psychiatric hospitals and prisons for over 30 years. She is co-editor/co-writer of several books, including two titles in the series Oxford Specialist Handbooks in Psychiatry, *Forensic Psychiatry* (with Nigel Eastman *et al.*; Oxford University Press, 2012) and *Medical Psychotherapy* (with Jessica Yakeley; Oxford University Press, 2016). With Dr Jay Sarkar, she co-edited *Clinical Topics in Personality Disorder* (Royal College of Psychiatrists, 2012), which won the BMA psychiatry book prize in 2013. She has been editor of the Forensic Focus series at Jessica Kingsley Publishers since 1998.

27

Chinese Medicine

A Journey from the Fringes

CHARLES C. BUCK

As a youthful new-ager in the 1970s reading the books of the moment – Fritzof Capra's *Tao of Physics*, the *Laozi* and Alan Watts's *Way of Zen* – I found myself wandering eastwards while trying to wrestle wisdom from China's ancient 'Book of Changes', the *Yijing*. On the Tibetan borderlands in 1979 I recalled the enthusiasm that one of my university medical physiology professors had expressed in the mid-1970s for acupuncture research and this prompted a search through the bookshops of New Delhi for books on this subject. I found only one, a slim volume by Dr Felix Mann called *Acupuncture: The Ancient Chinese Art of Healing*. Later, in Mumbai, I found a book by the Japanese acupuncture master Yoshio Manaka.

Reading these, it dawned on me that the 'wisdom of the East' thing was not only about philosophising with bearded guru-types or simply *doing nothing*; there might also be actual practical applications of all this stuff in the more gritty world of medicine. What if one could combine a youthful love of exotic orientalism with a lifelong love of clinical and medical science? So, back home in the UK, I sought out every book in print on the subject, and by 1980 I had obtained about nine – taking up 20cm of shelf space.

Cautious at first, this quest led me to an obscure netherworld and to a dingy shop called East Asia Bookstore behind London's Euston station (later transformed into the more glitzy Acumedic store on Camden High Street). An old shop bell on a spring *dinged* as I ventured into a strange and unfamiliar world. With brown linoleum with the pattern worn off, the East Asia Bookstore was lit by a green fluorescent tube and was the only acupuncture shop in the UK. Behind a glass cabinet containing what appeared to be some very specialist sado-masochist equipment stood the smiling acu-entrepreneur and pioneer Benny Mei. I was about to experience the hand of fortune.

Very few books change your life in this way, but here in this strange place I found the one that did this for me – an obscure collection of acupuncture research summaries, the proceedings of a conference held in Beijing in 1979. Remember, this was a time when China occupied a place in most people's minds that was roughly as distant and alien as the planet Mars is today. As a trained medical scientist I had, until now, hesitated to spend three years in self-funded study at a private college for fear of investing in a delusion. Now I realised that the genius of China's ancient scholars was not just for fun: it had been researched. Here was 'alternative' medicine that had some real science to support it – even then.

This book was the clincher; I signed up straight away for the only extensive, full-time acupuncture training available in Europe at the time. Hooked, from that moment on I bought every acupuncture and Chinese medicine text as soon as it appeared in print – and continued to do this until it eventually became impossible to keep up. This was a profession in rapid advance.

One method we might use to gauge progress towards increasing recognition is to scope the literature, and also to track changes in its academic level. Doing these things also gives us a measure of the seriousness and achievements of the authors and the concerns of the profession. So this is what I offer in my blog today. Luckily for you I am not compelled to create long and meticulous lists; instead I will simply use a tape measure and this vague and inaccurate graph:

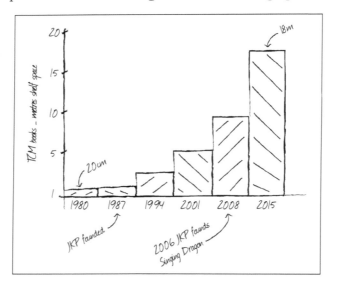

In 35 years we have seen exponential increases in the scholarly level of authors, and the depth of analysis. The pioneering authors rarely had the skills needed to directly access writings in Chinese and, for the most part, sources went unrecorded. Opinion was often presented as fact.

Some credit for the remarkable advancement of my profession must go to the publishers themselves. From around 1990 heavyweight publishers such as Longmans-Churchill Livingstone, Thieme and Springer-Verlag started to take an interest. Professional editorial quality control is a significant force for good – serious publishers avoid flakiness; they like to publish serious experts and obtain peer perspectives before sinking cash into projects. In this way publishers function as drivers to higher professional standards.

Jessica Kingsley Publishers has been respected for its publishing across health, social care, education and related professions since it started out in 1987, but in 2006 Jessica Kingsley herself founded a new imprint to JKP, Singing Dragon, dedicated to publishing titles on acupuncture, classical Chinese medicine and the traditional healing arts and related subjects. The Singing Dragon imprint became quickly established as a serious player, with Jessica actively commissioning much of the new list. She then struck gold when she recruited Claire Wilson, an experienced commissioning editor previously working in acupuncture and Chinese medicine for Longmans-Churchill-Livingstone, who has helped to further develop its publishing.

Taking books as a measure, the growth of the acupuncture and Chinese medicine profession has been remarkable. Ultimately, though, the impact has been very much broader than just an increase in bound and printed paper. Modern medicine has begun to embrace the wisdom of ancient China. Critics of acupuncture used to say, 'Maybe you're OK with blocked noses but you wouldn't be much use in the Emergency Room – ha ha!' How times change! Emergency rooms in Israel, Australia and the US now employ acupuncturists to treat acute pain, and the US Army uses acupuncture for battlefield care. The world of medicine has changed in ways that were once unimaginable. I feel so fortunate to have stumbled into this very satisfying medical field and to have been present at the birth of serious acupuncture and Chinese medicine study in the West. Assisted by pioneering publishers, we have seen its move from the fringes to the mainstream and from exotic oriental fad to genuine healthcare. I congratulate Jessica Kingsley Publishers on their thirtieth anniversary and thank them for the great contribution they continue to make to our profession.

* * *

CHARLES C. BUCK is an experienced clinician, educator and author on acupuncture and Chinese medicine with diverse interests including medical sciences and the practice of classical oriental medicine. An ex-Chairman of the British Acupuncture Council, he has practised in Chester for 34 years and has lectured extensively for most of this time. More details at www.charles-buck.com

28

Chinese Medicine in the West

NIGEL CHING

Chinese medicine has experienced exponential growth in the West during the past 30 years. It has gone from being an esoteric fringe therapy practised by a few dedicated pioneers, to being widely available and commonly utilised by the general population.

Whereas 30 years ago most ordinary members of the public had no personal experience of acupuncture or Chinese herbs, most people now have either tried acupuncture themselves or at least know someone who has. In some countries acupuncture has also taken the leap from something taught on weekend courses to becoming a Masters level programme, with people even attaining PhDs in the field.

Chinese medicine has also transgressed the boundaries of being seen exclusively as a 'quack therapy' that doctors warned their patients against trying as it was at best useless or at worst harmful, to being a therapy that has been integrated into certain fields of conventional Western medicine. There are, for example, ever-increasing numbers of Western healthcare practitioners such as physiotherapists and midwives, as well as some dentists and GPs, utilising acupuncture techniques in their daily practice. This is something that, if not unthinkable, seemed at least highly improbable 30 years ago.

There is though a significant risk of some of the tools of Chinese medicine, for example the techniques of acupuncture, cupping (applying special cups to an area to create a vacuum) and the herbs utilised in Chinese herbal medicine, being purloined and integrated into Western medicine while at the same time becoming divorced from the theoretical framework that is their foundation, the practical application of these tools being explained and defined by Western medicine's theoretical model. This will result in a significant loss, as the strength of Chinese medicine lies not only in its techniques, but also in the medical system itself, its unique comprehension of physiology, aetiology and pathology, and its understanding that an individual factor, whether it be a pathological symptom or a healing technique, can never be fully comprehended unless it is seen as part of a context.

Furthermore we are also seeing a concerted attempt from certain quarters of the academic and medical community not only to discredit the practice and practitioners of Chinese medicine, but also to pressurise the academic institutions that offer or accredit programmes in acupuncture and Chinese medicine to terminate their association with what they term 'pseudoscience', as well as opposing the use of acupuncture in public healthcare. However, I think that the profession is robust enough, and the demand from the public for a safe and effective alternative to biomedicine is great enough, that the profession will continue to grow in the years to come.

There has not only been a dynamic development in the usage and acceptance of Chinese medicine in the West during the past 30 years. The profession itself has also developed and matured. This professional development is most clearly seen in the difference between the relatively sparse literature that was available 30 years ago and the cornucopia of texts on the market today. I was lucky to start in the profession in 1990 when the first literary wave of Chinese medicine textbooks had already rolled onto the beach. I had access to books such as Maciocia's *Foundations of Chinese Medicine* (2015) and Kaptchuk's *The Web that Has No Weaver* (2000), two books that introduced a new level of erudition to the West, something the generation before had not had. This earlier generation, who were now starting to write books of their own, had mainly been dependent on translations of the standard textbooks available in China in the late seventies and early eighties. These pioneers were instrumental in developing the profession and setting its standards.

Even though when I started I had access to these seminal textbooks, there was still a paucity of textbooks compared to now. There would be a period of months between new related titles being published. I remember eagerly awaiting the publication of each coming addition to my meagre library. As Chinese medicine developed in the West, the amount of writing and the number of Chinese medicine textbooks published grew. Within ten years, so many books were being published that I could not keep up and felt guilty that I had not read each new tome.

Now, almost 30 years after I started out, we are in the fortunate but also frustrating situation that literally dozens of Chinese medicine textbooks are published each year without me or other practitioners and students even being aware of their existence. This is, of course, unfortunate for the individual authors and publishers, but it is a sign of the rude health and maturity of the profession – that there is a market for all these books. A further salubrious sign is that it is not just the volume but also the quality, depth and diversity of publications which has increased.

Looking back at the first books, they were very broad and general in scope and heavily influenced by the modern standard version of Chinese medicine known as 'TCM' (Traditional Chinese Medicine). Now there are in-depth textbooks focusing on virtually every specialised area of treatment, for example trauma, fertility, mental health, and so on. Equally inspiring, and a sign of the way that the profession has developed, is the publication of more and more books that diverge from the 'mainstream' modern TCM version of Chinese medicine. There is, for example, an increasing number of high-quality translations of classical historical texts, as well as textbooks on other traditions within East Asian medicine. This is proof that Chinese medicine in the West has matured. It is like a child who has reached adolescence and maturity, defining its own identity and seeking out its own truths; respectful to its parent, but also having attained a position of maturity and knowledge that enables it to be able to define itself independently, with its own views and opinions.

This is fully in the tradition of Chinese medicine and Chinese culture. Each generation is a transverse thread, weaving itself through the longitudinal threads of life's tapestry. Each individual weft thread may vary in colour, but they are still interwoven into the original tapestry. The Chinese medical profession in the West has come of age. I think the coming decades will see Chinese medicine in the West continuing to develop its own unique identity and expression, but it will always be clearly recognisable as a child of its mother.

References

Kaptchuk, T. (2000) *Chinese Medicine: The Web that Has No Weaver.* London: Random House. (Originally published as *The Web that Has No Weaver.*)

Maciocia, G. (2015) *Foundations of Chinese Medicine.* Amsterdam: Elsevier.

* * *

NIGEL CHING, who lives and practises in Copenhagen, has been a practitioner of Chinese medicine for nearly 30 years. Nigel has an MSc in Chinese medicine and has published two books in English, *The Fundamentals of Acupuncture* (Singing Dragon, 2016) and *The Art and Practice of Diagnosis* (Singing Dragon, 2017), as well as three acupuncture textbooks in Danish. Nigel is course director at the Nordic Acupuncture College in Copenhagen and regularly lectures internationally.

29

Yoga Therapy

A Pleasant Surprise

MATTHEW TAYLOR

Jessica Kingsley Publishers began 30 years ago. Had a futurist then predicted that yoga would be leading a shift in health behavior around the world in 2017, they would have been laughed out of the room. Yoga, did you say 'yogurt'? Remember that old response?

Well yoga, and yoga therapy in particular, is making a difference in health behavior today in what creativity researcher Jerome Bruner (1997) coined as an 'effective surprise' emerging out of the complexity of human behavior. That is, initially the idea (that yoga can create healthy behavioral changes) sounds surprising, but then fairly rapidly transitions to 'Well of course!' in its acceptance level in society. That is exactly where we find ourselves today. Allow me to explain how we got here and why JKP has been an important participant in fostering the evolution of the future of yoga therapy.

My perspective is based on studying yoga therapy for 20 years, watching the research on it emerge and participating in its emergence, and having led the International Association of Yoga Therapists (IAYT; www. iayt.org). Yoga initially received some exposure in Europe and the US in the early twentieth century, followed by a larger introduction as a part of the social changes in the 1960s, but then fell into dormancy, or what may better be termed a 'gestation', until the early 1990s. During that period schools in India and teachers in the West were quietly developing in ways that would come to fill a need in modern society. The entry point for the average student was via a physical practice as a new form of exercise, but the core of teachers and leaders appreciated that there was something much more that was available through a yoga practice than just a physical fitness routine. This core group, and some fair number of their students, had experienced not just physical benefits, but the transformative psychospiritual benefits of yoga as well.

These benefits were appreciated as being therapeutic, and in 1989 a small group of northern Californian teachers founded IAYT; around the world smaller groups were beginning to organize around the shared idea about the therapeutic benefits of yoga. This delineation of yoga therapy as distinct from yoga is a late-twentieth-century development. The reasons are many and complex, beyond the scope of this chapter. Generally speaking, yoga therapy includes a therapeutic relationship between the therapist and the student. This includes significantly more training beyond yoga, to include therapeutic ethics, interacting with the healthcare team of the student, an understanding of the related medical challenges, and defined limits of practice that aren't present in a standard yoga teaching relationship (see Blashki 2016).

Fast-forward to today and you can probably buy a book or DVD on yoga to address most ailments, from bunions to existential dread. Yoga is a mushrooming industry both as a service and as a marketplace for material goods. Executives do breathing exercises to start board meetings, and yoga pants apparently make people go shopping and travel as every store and airplane is full of people wearing yoga gear. With this cultural immersion and acceptance, many of the purveyors of yoga have co-opted yoga into a commodity to be sold. In therapeutic application yoga is being taught as another mechanistic modality prescription: Do these three asana, a side of pranayama (breathing exercises) thrice daily and call me next week. And run if someone at a party declares that they have achieved enlightenment in their yoga practice! If they have to declare it, this is a sure sign they haven't reached enlightenment, and that includes your beloved teacher. True adepts don't need to.

So what's happened to that 'something much more' that the leaders had identified early on? It turns out that yoga practitioners are changing their health behaviors and consuming fewer sick-care services. They are also seeking services from unconventional sources, including yoga studios, 'name-the-disease' support centers (e.g. Arthritis Support Group, The Lung Association, Cancer Support, etc.), halfway and safe houses, school gyms, homeless shelters, military bases, courthouses, craft brew pubs, and prison recreational centers. Why? This shift in venues is happening because practitioners are changing their lives and fostering new lifestyle habits.

And how do consumers and health professionals sort fact from fantasy from these observed behavioral changes in the yoga communities listed above in this age of misinformation and hyper-marketing? One way is by contributing to the knowledge base of science, such as the International Association of Yoga Therapists' PubMed indexed research journal, the *International Journal of Yoga Therapy*. Findings are also being published by related research, including the work of psychologist Richard Davidson, founder and chair of the Center for Healthy Minds (https://centerhealthyminds.org), where four main themes have developed in rigorous neuroscience demonstrating postive effects on wellbeing through human contemplative practices, primarily meditation, a subset of yoga that would have been considered New Age science fiction 20 years ago (Davidson 2015). These themes are:

1. Yoga-related practices create epigenetic changes (how your genes function).

2. Mind–body bi-directionality is real (mind changes body and body changes mind) in an expanding web of relationship between mind, body, microbiome and environment. Historically the mind was seen as the single operator of the machine-like body, with the body not influencing the mind. The idea of the microbiome (the trillions of microbes in your body which don't share your DNA but make up 90% of the cells you call 'your' body) influencing both mind and body was pure heresy. Now all three are understood to have shared roles in wellbeing (O'Donnell 2016).

3. Neuroplastic change in the human nervous system is possible to an increasingly greater level through contemplative and rehabilitation practices, contrary to the historic perspective that there was no capacity for change in an adult human nervous system (i.e. what you had can't and won't change).

4. Finally, these various contemplative practices increase the demonstrated human capacity and preference for pro-social behavior.

Are the big publishing houses first out to share this information? Hardly. However, browse the catalogues of Jessica Kingsley Publishers and their Singing Dragon imprint and you will find lists of publications that responsibly cover yoga as a health change agent. The book *Scoliosis, Yoga Therapy and the Art of Letting Go* (2016), written by my colleague Rachel Krentzman, a physiotherapist, is about far more than straightening spines in the entangled Middle East. She does offer solid instruction for stabilizing posture, but the real depth of her yoga therapy is 'letting go' of habits of mind to nurture healthier relationships with our self and others, to include the deep twists of societal relationships such as those in her current home in Israel. The mind extends far beyond our skin and crooked spines, to include the interpersonal relationships that define our lives (Siegel 2017). Likewise, my forthcoming book *Teaching from the Wisdom of Pain: Yoga Therapy as a Creative Response* (Taylor 2018) addresses moving in the world with persistent pain, but in creative ways built on the emerging science noted above, as well as that of transformative learning theory and creativity research. I have watched the 'miracles' of transformed lives through yoga therapy with patients suffering the most chronic, complex pain challenges, and more recently as veterans teach yoga to other veterans (see the Veterans Yoga Project at www.veteransyogaproject.org), healing both the teacher and the students. Yoga just keeps surprising!

This is how I think Jessica Kingsley Publishers fulfil their tagline of 'Books that Make a Difference'.

In this age of commodification and the search for quick profits, responsible publishing on health issues requires a publisher that:

- takes risks with progressive authors because the 'edge' is where change happens

- understands that to 'make a difference', they need to provide a voice to authors for audiences that often get overlooked

- invests in upfront vetting for the efficacy and impact of potential authors

- sustains a high level of integrity instead of chasing the next shiny object.

In standing by integrity and pursuing flexibility over the past 30 years, I congratulate JKP on demonstrating clarity and steadiness of heart–mind, while moving with the world, like a good yoga practitioner. Which in closing makes one wonder: what pleasant surprises are in store with yoga therapy and JKP in the next 30 years?

Stay tuned – none of us can even imagine! May we all work together, because *heyam dukham anagatam*, or:

'Future suffering can be avoided'

Yoga Sutra II.16

References

Blashki, L. (2016) 'Introduction to the IAYT Scope of Practice.' IAYT. www.iayt.org/page/IntroScope (accessed 17 July 2017).

Bruner, J. (1997) *On Knowing: Essays for the Left Hand*, second edition. Boston, MA: Belknap Press.

Davidson, R. (2015, 30 March) Wellbeing is a Skill [Video file]. www.youtube. com/watch?v=EPGJU7W0N0I (accessed 19 July 2017).

Krentzman, R. (2016) *Scoliosis, Yoga Therapy and the Art of Letting Go.* London: Singing Dragon.

O'Donnell, E. (2016) 'Readying for slings, arrows: Davidson lectures on benefits of meditation.' National Institutes of Health. https://nihrecord.nih.gov/ newsletters/2016/07_01_2016/story2.htm (accessed 17 July 2017).

Siegel, D. (2017) *Mind: A Journey to the Heart of Being Human.* New York: W. W. Norton & Co.

Taylor, M. (2018) *Teaching from the Wisdom of Pain: Yoga Therapy as a Creative Response.* London: Jessica Kingsley Publishers.

* * *

MATTHEW TAYLOR, PT, PhD, C-IAYT, has been a leader in integrative rehabilitation for over 20 years. Originally trained as a physical therapist, he later became a yoga therapist, culminating in his doctoral degree focused on yoga-based care for chronic spine pain. He led foundational work for the development of the profession of yoga therapy as past-president of the International Association of Yoga Therapists. Presently he is an author, researcher and philanthropist, having retired from clinical practice in 2016 after 35 years. Matthew has written numerous peer-reviewed professional journal articles and textbook chapters, is the editor of the textbook *Fostering Creativity in Rehabilitation* (Nova, 2015), and is writing *Teaching from the Wisdom of Pain: Yoga Therapy as a Creative Response* for Singing Dragon, which is due out in early 2018.

30

Aromatherapy Literature 1987–2017

JENNIFER PEACE RHIND

In 1987, aromatherapy was at the cusp of a phase of rapid growth in the UK. It was the year that I undertook my first formal studies, and in those days, aromatherapy was associated with beauty therapy, and indeed most practitioners were from that profession.

There were three books on my shelf: Jean Valnet's *The Practice of Aromatherapy*, the influential work of a French doctor who pioneered the use of essential oils in healing and clinical practices; Robert Tisserand's *Art of Aromatherapy*, a wonderful, eclectic and inspiring mix of approaches to practice from the esoteric to the clinical; and Marguerite Maury's *The Secret of Life and Youth*, the seminal work from the 'mother of aromatherapy', whose holistic perspective was infused with Tibetan traditional medicine, and focused on the external use of essential oils accompanied by massage. It is worth mentioning these texts; they became 'classics' because they all influenced the development of aromatherapy education and practice in English-speaking countries.

Aromatherapy has many facets – it is a therapy based on the use of essential oils and other aromatic plant extracts, encompassing olfaction as well as the pharmacological effects of the oils via inhalation and transdermal absorption – and so it is inherently complex. This is compounded by its rich and colourful history; aromatics have been used for healing the body and spirit since time immemorial, and across the globe. Aromatherapy writers and practitioners embraced healing philosophies from the East and the West, as well as the more reductionist biomedical models, to inform, underpin and explain practices. As a consequence, the literature became more diverse, reflecting the different directions that practitioners were taking.

In the 1990s and beyond, we began to witness big changes in the profession. Aestheticians remained focused on skin care, detoxification and relaxation, while nurse practitioner aromatherapists emerged. Aromatherapy began to take a more clinical stance, influenced by the French 'medical' approach and the growing emphasis on evidence-based practice. As the science/pharmacology aspects came to the fore, the softer 'aroma' part of the therapy receded. However, many believed that aromatherapy should be practised within a holistic context, and so, quietly and gently, and over the decades, a clearer picture of aromatherapy philosophy began to emerge – one that acknowledged its roots, branches and scope of practice.

There were always many books for the layperson – numerous 'how to' guides, often littered with dubious suggestions that ranged from the silly to the downright dodgy – but until the late 1990s there were very few texts aimed at professionals, many of whom were struggling to gain credibility because of the paucity of published evidence, the lack of a coherent philosophical basis and the quality of the prevailing literature.

Despite this, aromatherapy grew in popularity, training courses flourished, professional bodies and organisations became prominent and influential, and the numbers of practitioners increased – and of course so did the literature, which began to improve in quality and offer a deeper and broader perspective of the therapy. Aromatherapy was regarded as an effective complementary intervention in many areas – including pain, mental health and stress – and as a consequence, essential oils became the focus of many investigations across a range of disciplines. So, over the next two decades, authors had an ever-expanding source of life and social science research to draw upon to support their work, much of which verified traditional as well as contemporary aromatherapy practices, such as the use of essential oils to positively influence mood or to relieve pain and inflammation.

This welcome injection of some robust research did much to support the clinical aspects of aromatherapy, which had diversified into many strands such as cancer care, care of the elderly, dementia, palliative care, skin care, mental health, fertility, pregnancy and maternity care, sports therapy and sports injuries, and musculoskeletal and nervous system disorders – to name but a few!

Research was also elucidating the possible modes of action of essential oils, highlighting their promise in specific clinical settings, notably pain relief, respiratory disorders, dermatology, anxiety and depression, and infection control. From the Western, biomedical perspective, aromatherapy was growing in stature. Despite this, many therapists asserted that something was missing, that something had been lost in the quest for acceptance by the medical and allied professions. What of traditional wisdom, which points to aromatic potential yet to be explored, what about the psychosensory perspective where we use aroma to enhance, modify or stabilise cognitive and emotional states, and what about the vitalistic philosophies which acknowledge the role of non-physical influences on our health and wellbeing, that made our therapy so distinct and vibrant in the early days?

Aromatherapy literature reflected this dichotomy: scientific or esoteric? We had books firmly rooted in the clinical domain, and others that explored the intangible world of the spirit. However, what is so special in the world of aromatherapy is that our authors began to blend science with traditional knowledge, observation and intuition to create a new aromatherapy philosophy – one that is both holistic and evidence based, and with a vitalistic element. We have come a very long way from the three classic books on my 1987 bookshelf, via a plethora of popular literature that served to fuel the growth in aromatherapy, some authoritative texts for clinical practice, and some innovative authors who offered us insights into traditional modalities and their relevance to aromatherapy practice. The finest example of aromatherapy literature to date is Peter Holmes' *Aromatica*, a clinical manual for professionals which seamlessly incorporates therapeutics with energetics and is the classic text for the new era.

So, where now? There is no doubt that some of the existing literature will be expanded into further editions, because each and every week research is published that offers new knowledge and possibilities. Aromatherapists can learn a lot from folk medicine and ethnopharmacology, and thus books have yet to be written about their relevance to our practice. The sense of smell is at the heart of aromatherapy, but there is a rich seam of fragrance research that has yet to be explored from our specific perspective – and what about therapeutic perfumery, where essential oil-based scents can be 'tailor made' for an individual with the purpose of eliciting specific therapeutic effects, taking into account personal reactions and underpinned by published evidence? Our senses are the interface between ourselves and the environment, and indeed the non-physical realms. When we align our sense of smell with meditation and mindfulness, we can gain insights into the energetic qualities of our aromatics, adding another layer, another dimension to our practice.

We need writers to walk this path too. It would be safe to say that there are many more illuminating books just waiting to be written.

* * *

JENNIFER PEACE RHIND has a background in the biological sciences and education, and a longstanding interest in aromatic plants, ethnomedicine, flavour, fragrance and perfumery. She has published several books with Singing Dragon, including *Essential Oils: A Handbook for Aromatherapy Practice* (2012), *Fragrance and Wellbeing* (2014), *Listening to Scent* (2014) and *Aromatherapeutic Blending: Essential Oils in Synergy* (2016).

Developments in Shiatsu Over the Past 30 Years

CAROLA BERESFORD-COOKE

Shiatsu is a Japanese bodywork therapy derived from the traditional Chinese medical model which includes the points and meridians of acupuncture, but which has over its long history happily absorbed other therapies, Eastern and Western, and contributed to many more. Variants of 'pressure point massage' exist under different names all over the Far East. Shiatsu, which means 'finger pressure' in Japanese, is one of them; pressure can be applied with knees, thumbs, elbows and palms as well as fingers. It is characterised by relaxed leaning of the practitioner's body weight on the (clothed) receiver's meridian lines and acupuncture points, rather than forceful pressure, a technique which requires skill and sensitivity as well as relaxation. Skill is also required in the sensing of the correct lines, points and areas to treat, resulting in a deep yet comfortable sensation for the receiver. Shiatsu is suitable for all ages and is traditionally considered as a way of maintaining health and preventing disease, while also helpful for a number of ailments of mind and body.

By 1987 Shiatsu had already achieved the move from its homeland in Japan to establish thriving communities in the West. The most successful of these was in the UK, where common law allowed willing patients to be treated by non-doctor complementary and alternative medicine (CAM) practitioners, subject to minor legal limitations. In many European countries whose laws were still based on the Napoleonic Code, specific legislation was required to allow non-doctor CAM therapists to practise. (There is a deep-rooted incompatibility between English common law, which specifies things that are not allowed but tolerates much else, and the Napoleonic Code, which lists things that *are* allowed, and anything else is illegal.)

America's circumstances were different, partly because of its vast size and federal nature, and partly because Shiatsu had entered the US directly from Japan, across the Pacific. It was practised mainly by Japanese masseurs, many of whom had qualified at the Japan Shiatsu College – which is, and has been since the recognition of Shiatsu by the Japanese government in 1964, the only college in Japan permitted to give its graduates a licence to practise. The college's style is strongly influenced by Western anatomical theory and the traditional concept of meridians, and other classical aspects of the theory are absent. Practitioners of this style, as immigrants, often had to work in massage parlours and spas, and in consequence Shiatsu had limited opportunity to elevate its profile.

In 1987 the UK Shiatsu community was feeling especially good about itself. Shiatsu was among the best known of the 'alternative therapies', with an abundance of prosperous clients eager to lie down and pay to be relaxed and healed. The UK Shiatsu Society was the envy of the alternative world, with a constitution, rules and regulations, and relatively little internecine strife. New schools offering ongoing professional trainings were beginning to be established, with teachers who were clear what they were teaching and keen to impart their knowledge, whether it was derived from a study of acupuncture (allowed in the UK to non-doctors) or macrobiotic theory, the only other complementary practices at that time with a theory similar to Shiatsu.

Looking back over the past 30 years is a humbling experience. The confidence of the burgeoning therapy has taken some hard knocks in order to mature into a degree of self-knowledge. In the face of sceptical inquiry, Shiatsu has had to question itself: Is it bodywork? Is it healing? Is it 'acupuncture without needles'? How is modern Shiatsu in the West related to its origins in Japan, and to the many other Asian bodywork therapies derived ultimately from ancient Chinese medical practice? How can modern science throw light on the experiences and healing results that come to both practitioner and client? In seeking to answer these questions the therapy has begun to understand its potential.

Shiatsu, uniquely, sees itself as a therapy in which the practitioner is duty-bound to recognise the importance of their participation. In giving Shiatsu, the practitioner engages in a process in which their own responses to what is happening are as important as the responses of the receiver, and guide the session as much as any pre-determined protocol. Enriched by the Japanese tradition of including physical and psychological self-development as a part of the training, Shiatsu encourages each individual to reference their intuition as well as the classical theory. Shiatsu can call on the unifying theory that generated acupuncture and Chinese herbal medicine, and that is the foundation of the Asian model of a healthy lifestyle, but does not need to follow slavishly the rules laid down over centuries by the literature of acupuncture. The unique approach of each practitioner (and teacher) is recognised as an asset rather than a source of discord. The UK Shiatsu community did once envisage bringing the different approaches into universal agreement as an achievable goal, but fell into political strife, now thankfully ended. Shiatsu therapists no longer try to fit the client into a uniform 'box' of diagnosis, prognosis and treatment protocol because they recognise that each of them will respond to the client in a different way and thus create a different session.

Over the past 30 years the attitude of the public has also changed. Clients are now clearer about what they want and more realistic in their expectations. They are more wary of self-professed healers – and practitioners are now limited by law in what success they are allowed to claim. The public has a much wider knowledge of the different therapies available to them, and clients are often experienced in receiving them. Most notably, people are keen to support their own health with diet, exercise and mindfulness techniques in a way that would have been considered eccentric and self-obsessed 30 years ago.

This development has encouraged the Shiatsu community to strengthen its links with its sources in ancient Chinese medical theory, which includes dietary remedies and different forms of exercise, tailored to each individual with awareness of subtleties of circumstance and constitution, as part of a practical, holistic approach to health. As well as working to support the client's self-healing power with bodywork, the practitioner can offer lifestyle changes which will carry that healing process forward into the future.

Shiatsu's flexible nature, partaking of the techniques, both Eastern and Western, that have influenced it throughout its history, has been acknowledged. There is wider co-operation between Shiatsu communities worldwide, which increases the diversity of styles. In all this diversity, what holds Shiatsu together as a recognisable therapy is the practice of surrendering to gravity, the simple act of leaning, trustingly, with relaxation, on another human being. Attendant on this are other processes – the practice of non-doing, simply aligning ourselves with the natural ways of being, expansion and relaxation, that are our neglected birthright. This is the real basis of Shiatsu, a profound discovery of our shared humanity for both giver and receiver, and one that makes Shiatsu deeply loved.

As we have become more fluent in expressing our explorations of our interior worlds, these experiences are put into words more confidently in the growing body of Shiatsu literature. In expressing them, we free ourselves from perceived needs to conform to Chinese medical theory; this in turn allows us to re-visit our understanding of that theory and express it freshly in terms suitable for our own culture, without losing sight of the responses we share with Asian – and all – cultures. The understanding is no longer lost in translation from East to West but becomes our common heritage.

A new Shiatsu literature is in the process of evolving, in papers given at conferences or articles in professional journals, which puts experience rather than formulae at its core, allowing a voice to the philosophical, the practical, the spiritual, the humorous aspects of our practice, and showing a new self-knowledge in our therapy that enables us to connect more wisely and supportively with our receivers and each other.

* * *

CAROLA BERESFORD-COOKE has been practising Shiatsu since 1978, with a brief detour into acupuncture studies in order to learn more about Shiatsu. She was present at the founding of the UK Shiatsu Society in 1981 and in 1986 co-founded the Shiatsu College, one of the major UK training schools. Her published works include *The Book of Massage* (Shiatsu section; Ebury Press, 1990), *Acupressure* (Naturally Better series; Ramboro Books, 1997), and *Shiatsu Theory and Practice*, republished in 2016 by Singing Dragon.

Printed in Great Britain
by Amazon